AFPC

PRACTICE & REVISION KIT

Paper G10

Taxation and Trusts

(Finance Act 2004)

This **Practice and Revision** Kit contains:

- **Advice on exam technique** which is essential to ensure that you are prepared for the exam.

- Both **short form** and **case study questions** providing ample opportunity to practise application skills and ensure exam success.

- **Key facts** highlighting the required knowledge for this exam, enabling you to identify and remedy weaknesses.

- **Two mock exams** ensure your final preparation is focused on the task in hand – success.

SUBJECT UPDATES ARE AVAILABLE ON OUR WEBSITE AT: www.bpp.com/afpc

BPP Professional Education
July 2004

First edition 2000
Sixth edition July 2004

ISBN 0 7517 1714 2 (previous edition 07517 1208 6)

British Library Cataloguing-in-Publication Data
A catalogue record for this book
is available from the British Library

Published by

BPP Professional Education
Aldine House, Aldine Place
London W12 8AW

www.bpp.com

Printed in Great Britain by W M Print
45-47 Frederick Street
Walsall, West Midlands
WS2 9NE

We are grateful to the Chartered Insurance Institute for permission to reproduce in this Kit references to the syllabus of which the Institute holds the copyright

CONTENTS

INTRODUCTION

Welcome to BPP's FA 2004 AFPC Practice & Revision Kit

You're taking professional exams. You're under time pressure to get your exam revision done. And trying to fit in study as well as a social life around your job is difficult. Could you make better use of your time? Are you sure that your revision is really relevant to the exam you will be facing?

If you use BPP revision material you can be sure that the time you spend revising and practising questions is time well spent. Our **Practice & Revision Kits** are clear, concise and effective and are focused exclusively on what you, the candidate, can expect to encounter in your exam.

- We offer **guidance on revision, question practice and exam technique** gleaned from years of successfully helping students to pass their AFPC exams.

- We highlight the format of the exam that you will face and ensure that all of the **exam standard questions in the Kit** reflect that format.

- We ensure that **the bank of tutorial questions is comprehensive** so that you can cover all areas of the syllabus if you have time.

- We provide **Key Facts Checklists** which test your knowledge and understanding of syllabus areas and let you see whether or not you really are ready to begin practice and revision.

- We provide you with two **mock exams** to home your final preparation towards success. The exams are based on those set by the Institute and have been updated to Finance Act 2004 and amended where necessary to reflect the current syllabus. Model answers have been prepared by us.

REVISION AND PRACTICE SKILLS

How to revise

This is a very important time as you approach the exam. You must remember three things.

> **Use time sensibly**
> **Set realistic goals**
> **Believe in yourself**

Use time sensibly

1   **How much study time do you have?** Remember that you must EAT, SLEEP, and of course, RELAX.

2   **How will you split that available time between each subject?** What are your weaker subjects? They need more time.

3   **What is your learning style?** AM/PM? Little and often/long sessions? Evenings/ weekends?

4   **Are you taking regular breaks?** Most people absorb more if they do not attempt to study for long uninterrupted periods of time. A five minute break every hour (to make coffee, watch the news headlines) can make all the difference.

5   **Do you have quality study time?** Unplug the phone. Let everybody know that you're studying and shouldn't be disturbed.

Set realistic goals

1   Have you set a **clearly defined objective** for each study period?

2   Is the objective **achievable**?

3   Will you **stick to your plan**? Will you make up for any **lost time**?

4   Are you **rewarding yourself** for your hard work?

5   Are you leading a **healthy lifestyle**?

Believe in yourself

Are you cultivating the right attitude of mind? There is absolutely no reason why you should not pass this exam if you adopt the correct approach

- **Be confident** - you've passed exams before, you can pass them again

- **Be calm** - plenty of adrenaline but no panicking

- **Be focused** - commit yourself to passing the exam

Exam technique

Passing professional examinations is half about having the knowledge, and half about doing yourself full justice in the examination. You must have the right technique.

The day of the exam
---

1   Set at least one **alarm** (or get an alarm call) for a morning exam

2   Have **something to eat** but beware of eating too much; you may feel sleepy if your system is digesting a large meal

3   Allow plenty of **time to get to the exam hall**; have your route worked out in advance and listen to news bulletins to check for potential travel problems

4   **Don't forget** pens, pencils, rulers, erasers

5   Put **new batteries** into your calculator and take a spare set (or a spare calculator)

6   **Avoid discussion** about the exam with other candidates outside the exam hall

---
Technique in the exam hall
---

1   *Read the instructions (the 'rubric') on the front of the exam paper carefully*

Check that the exam format hasn't changed.

2   *Plan your attack carefully*

Be prepared to skip questions which seem difficult at first and move on to new questions. You will have time to come back later.

3   *Check the time allocation for each question*

Each mark carries with it a **time allocation** of approximately 1 minute (including time for selecting and reading questions). Be careful not to leave questions unanswered because you spent too long on certain questions. Monitor your time carefully.

4   *Read the question carefully and plan your answer*

Read through the question again very carefully when you come to answer it. Case study questions are rarely straightforward and it is easy to get the wrong answer as a result of poor reading. Take care.

5   *Answer every question*

If you don't know the answer, make an educated guess.

6   *Stay until the end of the exam*

Use any spare time **checking and rechecking** your answers.

7   *Don't worry if you feel you have performed badly in the exam*

It is more than likely that the other candidates will have found the exam difficult too. Don't forget that there is a competitive element in these exams. As soon as you get up to leave the exam hall, *forget* **that exam** and think about the next.

8   *Don't discuss an exam with other candidates*

This is particularly the case if you **still have other exams to sit**. Even if you have finished, you should put it out of your mind until the day of the results. Forget about exams and relax!

Practising questions

There are several Key Facts checklists. If you read through these revision topics and feel confident that you know what they are about, attempt the questions and monitor your performance.

The Mock Exams

You should attempt the papers under exam conditions, so that you gain experience of selecting and sequencing your questions, and managing your time. Applying our marking scheme will help you get an idea of how you will fare in your exam. Rework them until you are achieving a mark of around 80% to ensure you are well above the exam pass mark of around 55%.

REVISION STUDY PLAN

How to use the Revision Study Plan

For each phase you should start off revising with the Key Facts quiz, which will test whether you are familiar with the core areas of the syllabus. If you are not happy with your knowledge, you need to go back to the Study Text to consolidate your learning.

Next, attempt the short form questions shown for the phase. These show the type of question you may be asked in Section A of the Paper. Once again, go back to the Study Text if you are unsure whether you could answer these questions in the examination.

For some phases, there are 40 and 75 mark questions shown. These test topics covered in the phase you are working on **and in previous phases**. You must be prepared to answer questions dealing with aspects from different parts of the syllabus. This is particularly the case in 75 mark questions. Therefore, as your revision progresses, you should expect to attempt more longer questions.

The final two phases of your revision plan consist of two full mock examinations. You should attempt these under examination conditions. Solutions with full mark allocations are provided for you to self-mark your attempt. Be realistic, but not over critical.

REVISION STUDY PLAN

Phase	Key facts quiz	Done (✓)	SFQs no.	Done (✓)	40 mark questions	Done (✓)	75 mark questions	Done (✓)
1	Income tax basics		1 2 3 4					
2	Employment, self employment, benefits and tax credits		5 6 7 8		46. Mr K			
3	CGT basics		9 10 11 12		47. Jim Smith		57. Donald Manton	
4	CGT reliefs		13 14					
5	Overseas aspects of personal taxation		15 16					
6	IHT basics		17 18 19 20 21 22		48. Andy 49. Hawksbill 50. Ken Sing			
7	Additional aspects of IHT		23 24		51. Sebastian Worth 52. Len Shackleton			
8	Taxation of investments		25 26 27 28 29		53. Tannia Whiting 54. Sally and George			
9	Essentials of trusts and trustees		30 31 32					
10	Statutory and non-statutory trusts		33 34 35 36					
11	Tax on trusts and uses of trusts		37 38 39 40 41		55. Roy and Cybille 56. Bill Watts		58. Tom Jones 59. David Stamp 60. Keith and Ann	
12	Pensions; unit trusts; bankruptcy; and powers of attorney		42 43 44 45				61. Joe Pollard	
13	Mock exam 1							
14	Mock exam 2							

THE EXAM

Taxation and Trusts exam

The weighting of the exam is as follows.

Questions	Marks	%
Section A 5 - 7 short questions	45	22½%
Section B Compulsory case study	75	37½%
Section C 2 questions from 3	80	40%
	200	100%

The CII do not disclose a pass mark but it is generally considered that 55% would obtain a pass.

The exam itself consists of 200 marks and is set over 3 hours. A key requirement is to make sure that you *are* well-prepared, so that you can answer some of the questions quickly and give yourself more time for the ones you find more difficult. You will probably find the exam time-pressured.

Exam technique

1   **Preparation**
     -    A positive attitude will increase your performance by 10%.
     -    Practical preparation: you must do the mock exams and question practice.
     -    Revision: you must give yourself sufficient time to revise properly.

2   **Think and plan your answers**. Do not rush into writing down the first thing that comes into your head.
     -    Start by scanning the paper, do easiest question first, usually Section A.
     -    Read questions carefully, highlight the key words, e.g. LIST, DISCUSS.
     -    Answer the question set, not what you want to answer.
     -    Make plans.
     -    DO NOT GO OVER THE TIME ALLOCATION (0.9 minute per mark)
     -    Answer everything.
     -    BE PROFESSIONAL
          -    Show that you know a lot, be comprehensive and specific.
          -    Although there is no negative marking, don't make things up just to fill in space. Better to move on elsewhere.

3   **Marker's attitude**
    -   Be helpful, put yourself in their shoes.
    -   Your work must be comprehensible.
    -   Key points should be made first, before peripheral points.
    -   Justification of points is essential if there is any equivocation.

4   **The marking guide awards marks for the following.**
    -   Identification of major issues
    -   Appropriate and adequate analysis
    -   Adequate core knowledge demonstrated, technically sharp
    -   Sound judgement, recommendations are practical and commercial

5   **You can only present well if you plan and group like points together.**
    -   Use headings.
    -   Keep your statements short and snappy.
    -   Start each statement on a new line.
    -   If you have poor handwriting use alternate lines.
    -   Start each new part of the question on a separate sheet.
        -   It looks better.
        -   Allows you to come back later to enhance or complete.

BPP
PROFESSIONAL EDUCATION

TAX TABLES

Income tax rates

2003/04		2004/05	
Rate	Band	Rate	Band
%	£	%	£
10	1 -1,960	10	0 -2,020
22	1,961-30,500	22	2,021-31,400
40	Over 30,500	40	Over 31,400

National Insurance contributions: 2004/05 rates

	Weekly	Monthly	Yearly
Class I (employee)			
Lower Earnings Limit (LEL)	£79.00	£343.00	£4,108.00
Upper Earnings Limit (UEL)	£610.00	£2,644.00	£31,720.00
Earnings Threshold (ET)★	£91.00	£395.00	£4,745.00

Employees' contributions – Class 1

Total earnings £ per week	Contracted in rate	Contracted out rate
Below £91.00★	Nil	Nil
£91.01 - £610.00	11%	9.4%
Excess over £610.00	1%	1%
		1.6% rebate on earnings between LEL and ET

Employers' contributions – Class 1

Total earnings £ per week	Contracted-in rate	Contracted-out rate	
		Final salary	Money purchase
Below £91.00★	Nil	Nil	Nil
£91.01 - £610.00	12.8%	9.3%	11.8%
Excess over £610.00	12.8%	12.8%	12.8%
		3.5% rebate on earnings between LEL and ET	1% rebate on earnings between LEL and ET

★ Earnings threshold below which no NICs payable. There is a zero band between the lower earnings limit (£79 pw) and the earnings threshold (£91 pw) to protect lower earners' rights to contributory state benefits such as basic state pension.

Class 1A (employer's contributions on most benefits) 12.8% on all relevant benefits

Class II (self-employed) Flat rate per week £2.05 where earnings are over £4,215 pa

Class III (voluntary) Flat rate per week £7.15

Class IV (self-employed) 8% on profits £4,745 – £31,720; 1% on profits above £31,720

Income tax reliefs

		2003/04 £	2004/05 £
Personal allowance	– under 65	4,615	4,745
	– 65 – 74	6,610	6,830
	– 75 and over	6,720	6,950
Married couple's allowance	– 65 – 74 (see note 1)	5,565	5,725
	– 75 and over (see note 1)	5,635	5,795
	minimum for 65+	2,150	2,210
Age allowance income limit		18,300	18,900
Blind person's allowance		1,510	1,560
Enterprise investment scheme relief limit (see note 2)		150,000	200,000
Venture capital trust relief limit (see note 3)		100,000	200,000

Notes

1   Either spouse must be born before 6 April 1935. Relief is restricted to 10%.

2   EIS qualifies for 20% relief.

3   VCT qualifies for 20% tax relief in 2003/04 and 40% tax relief in 2004/05.

Working and child tax credits

Working tax credit	2003/04 £	2004/05 £
Basic element	1,525	1,570
Couple and lone parent element	1,500	1,545
30 hour element	620	640
Childcare element of WTC		
Maximum eligible cost for 1 child	135 per week	135 per week
Maximum eligible cost for 2 children	200 per week	200 per week
Percent of eligible child costs covered	70	70
Child tax credit		
Family element	545	545
Baby addition	545	545
Child element	1,445	1,625
Tax credits income		
Thresholds and withdrawal rates		
First income threshold	5,060	5,060
First withdrawal rate	37%	37%
Second income threshold	50,000	50,000
Second withdrawal rate	6.67%	6.67%
First threshold for those entitled to CTC	13,230	13,480
Income disregard	2,500	2,500

Personal Pension Contributions (PPCs) and Retirement Annuity Premiums (RAPs)

	% of Net Relevant Earnings	
Age at beginning of tax year	**PPCs** %	**RAPs** %
35 or less		17.5
	17.5	
36 – 45	20	17.5
46 – 50	25	17.5
51 – 55	30	
		20
56 – 60	35	22.5
61 or more	40	27.5

Earnings limit (PPCs only)		
	2004/05	£102,000
	2003/04	£99,000
	2002/03	£97,200
	2001/02	£95,400
	2000/01	£91,800
	1999/00	£90,600
	1998/99	£87,600
	1997/98	£84,000

Maximum contribution without evidence of earnings (2004/05) £3,600 gross (£2,808 net)

Car and fuel benefits

Company cars   Lower threshold CO_2 – 145g/km: 15% of list price (max £80,000 including VAT)

2004/05   Increase by 1% for each 5g/km (round down to nearest multiple of 5g)
3% supplement for diesel cars (maximum 35% of list price)
To maximum: 35% of list price (max £80,000 including VAT)

Car fuel   £14,400 ☐ % used for car benefit

Further information:

(a)   **In most cases, accessories** are included in the list price on which the benefit is calculated.

(b)   **List price** is reduced by employee's capital contributions (maximum £5,000).

(c)   **Car benefit** is reduced by the amount of employee's contributions towards running costs, but **fuel** benefit is reduced only if the employee makes good **all** the fuel used for private journeys.

Fixed profit car scheme (authorised mileage rates)

2004/05 rates

Car or Van		**Motorcycle**	24p
Up to 10,000 miles	40p	**Cycle**	20p
Over 10,000 miles	25p	**Passenger payments**	5p

Inheritance tax

Death rate %	Lifetime rate %	Chargeable 2004/05 £'000	Chargeable 2003/04 £'000	Chargeable 2002/03 £'000
Nil	Nil	0 – 263	0 – 255	0 – 250
40	20	Over 263	Over 255	Over 250

Reliefs

Annual exemption	£3,000	Marriage	– parent	£5,000
Small gifts	£250		– grandparent	£2,500
			– bride/groom	£2,500
			– other	£1,000

Reduced charge on gifts within 7 years of death

Years before death	0 – 3	3 – 4	4 – 5	5 – 6	6 – 7
% of death charge	100%	80%	60%	40%	20%

Main Social Security benefits

		From 7.4.03	From 12.4.04
		£	£
Child benefit	– first child	16.05	16.50
	– subsequent child	10.75	11.05
Incapacity benefit	– short term lower rate	54.40	55.90
	– short term higher rate	64.35	66.15
	– long term rate	72.15	74.15
Attendance allowance	– lower rate	38.30	39.35
	– higher rate	57.20	58.80
Retirement pension	– single	77.45	79.60
	– married	123.80	127.25
Widowed parent's allowance		77.45	79.60
Bereavement payment (lump sum)		2,000.00	2,000.00
Jobseekers allowance		54.65	55.65

Value added tax

Standard Rate	17½%
Annual Registration Limit – from 1 April 2004	£58,000
Deregistration Limit – from 1 April 2004	£56,000

Capital allowances

	First year allowance	Writing down allowance pa
Plant and machinery	40% *	25% (reducing balance)
Plant and machinery	50%**	25% (reducing balance)
Information and communication technology	100% ***	not usually applicable
Motor cars	–	25% (reducing balance) (max £3,000)
Motor cars – low emission (not more than 120gm/km)	100%	not usually applicable
Industrial buildings	–	4% (straight line)
Agricultural buildings	–	4% (straight line)
Hotels		4% (straight line)
Enterprise Zones	100%	–
Scientific research	100%	–
Patents, know-how	–	25% (reducing balance)

* For small and medium sized enterprises from 2 July 1998

** For small enterprises in the one year period commencing 1.4.04/6.4.04 (Companies/unincorporated businesses)
** For small enterprises from 1 April 2000 to 31 March 2004

Small/medium sized enterprises

	Turnover (not more than)	Balance sheet total (not more than)	No of employees (not more than)
Small enterprise	£5.6 million	£2.8 million	50
Medium sized enterprise	£22.8 million	£11.4 million	250

Capital gains tax

	2003/04	2004/05
Rate	Gains taxed at 10%, 20% or 40%, subject to level of income	Gains taxed at 10%, 20% or 40%, subject to level of income
Individuals-exemption	£7,900	£8,200
Trusts-exemption	£3,950	£4,100

Taper relief (for disposals on or after 6 April 2002)

Gains on business assets		Gains on non-business assets *	
Complete years after 5 April 98	% of gain chargeable	Complete years after 5 April 98	% of gain chargeable
0	100.0	0	100
1	50	1	100
2 or more	25	2	100
		3	95
		4	90
		5	85
		6	80
		7	75
		8	70
		9	65
		10 or more	60

* Non-business assets held on 17 March 1998 given additional year of relief.

Retail prices index

	Jan	Feb	Mar	Apr	May	Jun	Jul	Aug	Sep	Oct	Nov	Dec
1982			79.4	81.0	81.6	81.9	81.9	81.9	81.9	82.3	82.7	82.5
1983	82.6	83.0	83.1	84.3	84.6	84.8	85.3	85.7	86.1	86.4	86.7	86.9
1984	86.8	87.2	87.5	88.6	89.0	89.2	89.1	89.9	90.1	90.7	91.0	90.9
1985	91.2	91.9	92.8	94.8	95.2	95.4	95.2	95.5	95.4	95.6	95.9	96.0
1986	96.2	96.6	96.7	97.7	97.8	97.8	97.5	97.8	98.3	98.5	99.3	99.6
1987	100.0	100.4	100.6	101.8	101.9	101.9	101.8	102.1	102.4	102.9	103.4	103.3
1988	103.3	103.7	104.1	105.8	106.2	106.6	106.7	107.9	108.4	109.5	110.0	110.3
1989	110.0	111.8	112.3	114.3	115.0	115.4	115.5	115.8	116.6	117.5	118.5	118.8
1990	119.5	120.2	121.4	125.1	126.2	126.7	126.8	128.1	129.3	130.3	130.0	129.9
1991	130.2	130.9	131.4	133.1	133.5	134.1	133.8	134.1	134.6	135.1	135.6	135.7
1992	135.6	136.3	136.7	138.8	139.3	139.3	138.8	138.9	139.4	139.9	139.7	139.2
1993	137.9	138.8	139.3	140.6	141.0	141.0	140.7	141.3	141.9	141.8	141.6	141.9
1994	141.3	142.1	142.5	144.2	144.7	144.7	144.0	144.7	145.0	145.2	145.3	146.0
1995	146.0	146.9	147.5	149.0	149.6	149.8	149.1	149.9	150.6	149.8	149.8	150.7
1996	150.2	150.9	151.5	152.6	152.9	153.0	152.4	153.1	153.8	153.8	153.9	154.4
1997	154.4	155.0	155.4	156.3	156.9	157.5	157.5	158.5	159.3	159.5	159.6	160.0
1998	159.5	160.3	160.8	162.6	163.5	163.4	163.0	163.7	164.4	164.5	164.4	164.4
1999	163.4	163.7	164.1	165.2	165.6	165.6	165.1	165.5	166.2	166.5	166.7	167.3
2000	166.6	167.5	168.4	170.1	170.7	171.1	170.5	170.5	171.7	171.6	172.1	172.2
2001	171.1	172.0	172.2	173.1	174.2	174.4	173.3	174.0	174.6	174.3	173.6	173.4
2002	173.3	173.8	174.5	175.7	176.2	176.2	175.9	176.4	177.6	177.9	178.2	178.5
2003	178.4	179.3	179.9	181.2	181.5	181.3	181.3	181.6	182.5	182.6	182.7	183.5
2004	183.1	183.8	184.1									

Indexation relief was frozen at 5 April 1998 and replaced by taper relief for individuals and trustees.

Question bank
and
Key facts

KEY FACTS – INCOME TAX BASICS: QUESTIONS

- *Check that you can fill in the blanks in the statements below before you attempt any questions. If in doubt, you should go back to your BPP Study Text Chapter 1 and revise first.*

- An individual must submit his tax return for 2004/05 by ...., to avoid penalties being payable.

- Payments on account of income tax are required on .... and on ...., with a balancing payment on...

- Income from land and buildings (eg rents) are assessable under the rules of ....

- Schedule D Case I taxes ....

- Bank and building society interest is usually received ....

- Dividends are received with a .... tax credit.

- Income from National Savings Certificates is .... income tax.

- We need three columns in a personal tax computation, one each for .... income, ... income and .... income.

- In a personal income tax computation we must add up the individual's income from all sources and deduct charges to arrive at ...., and then deduct the personal allowance to arrive at ....

- Tax credits on UK dividends are .... to non-taxpayers.

- Where a husband and wife jointly own income-generating property, it is assumed that they are entitled to .... of the income

- Income produced by a gift from a parent to a child will be ....except if it ....

KEY FACTS – INCOME TAX BASICS: ANSWERS

- *Could you fill in the blanks? The answers are in bold. Use this page for revision purposes as you approach the exam.*

- An individual must submit his tax return for 2004/05 by **31 January 2006**, to avoid penalties being payable.

- Payments on account of income tax are required on **31 January in the tax year** and **on 31 July following the end of the tax year**, with a balancing payment on **31 January following the end of the tax year**.

- Income from land and buildings (eg. rents) are assessable under the rules of **Schedule A**.

- Schedule D Case I taxes **the profits of trades**.

- Bank and building society interest is usually received **net of 20% income tax**.

- Dividends are received with a **10%** tax credit.

- Income from National Savings Certificates is **exempt from** income tax.

- We need three columns in a personal tax computation, one each for **non-savings** income, **savings (excluding dividend)** income and **dividend** income.

- In a personal income tax computation we must add up the individual's income from all sources and deduct charges to arrive at **statutory total income**, and then deduct the personal allowance to arrive at **taxable income**.

- Tax credits on UK dividends are **not repayable** to non-taxpayers.

- Where a husband and wife jointly own income-generating property, it is assumed that they are entitled to **equal shares** of the income

- Income produced by a gift from a parent to a child will be **taxable on the parent** except if it **does not exceed £100 pa**.

KEY FACTS – EMPLOYMENT, SELF EMPLOYMENT, BENEFITS AND TAX CREDITS: QUESTIONS

- *Check that you can fill in the blanks in the statements below before you attempt any questions. If in doubt, you should go back to your BPP Study Text Chapters 2, 3 and 4 and revise first.*

- Income from employment is taxed on a .... basis.

- Expenses are, in general, deductible only if they are incurred ...., ... and .... in the performance of the duties of the employment.

- The general measure of a benefit for an employee earning £8,500 or more per annum or a director is the ....

- The taxable benefit for a car is list price x .... where the CO_2 emissions are less than 145g/km.

- There is a .... exemption on termination payments.

- Accommodation benefit can give rise to a taxable benefit for all employees. The basic benefit is .... and there is an additional benefit where the accommodation cost over ....

- The taxable benefit of assets made available for use by an employee is the higher of:

    (a)   ....% of the asset's ....; and
    (b)   any .... paid by the employer.

- But if a computer is made available to an employee, the first .... of benefit is exempt.

- The benefit assessable on the provision of a mobile phone is ....

- The usual basis period under Schedule D Cases I and II for a tax year is the period of account ending ....

- Capital allowances are deducted to arrive at ....

- Writing down allowance are available on .... at 25% per annum of the reducing balance.

- An employee is entitled to .... if he is sick for four or more days.

- National insurance retirement pension is based on sufficient Class .... or Class .... NICs. An individual can make voluntary Class .... NICs to make up any shortfall in her NIC record.

- Working tax credit is paid to an employee by the ....

- Child tax credit is paid by the .... to the ....

KEY FACTS - EMPLOYMENT, SELF EMPLOYMENT, BENEFITS AND TAX CREDITS: ANSWERS

- *Could you fill in the blanks? The answers are in bold. Use this page for revision purposes as you approach the exam.*

- Income from employment is taxed on a **receipts** basis.

- Expenses are, in general, deductible only if they are incurred **wholly, exclusively** and **necessarily** in the performance of the duties of the employment.

- The general measure of a benefit for an employee earning £8,500 or more per annum or a director is the **cost to the employer of providing it**.

- The taxable benefit for a car is list price x **15%** where the CO_2 emissions are less than 145g/km.

- There is a **£30,000** exemption on termination payments.

- Accommodation benefit can give rise to a taxable benefit for all employees. The basic benefit is **the annual value of the property** and there is an additional benefit where the accommodation cost over **£75,000**.

- The taxable benefit of assets made available for use by an employee is the higher of:

  (a)   **20**% of the asset's **market value;** and
  (b)   any **rent** paid by the employer.

- But if a computer is made available to an employee, the first **£500** of benefit is exempt.

- The benefit assessable on the provision of a mobile phone is **nil**.

- The usual basis period under Schedule D Cases I and II for a tax year is the period of account ending **in the tax year**.

- Capital allowances are deducted to arrive at **the Schedule D Case I or II profit**.

- Writing down allowance are available on **plant and machinery** at 25% per annum of the reducing balance.

- An employee is entitled to **statutory sick pay** if he is sick for four or more days.

- National insurance retirement pension is based on sufficient Class **1** or Class **2** NICs. An individual can make voluntary Class **3** NICs to make up any shortfall in her NIC record.

- Working tax credit is paid to an employee by the **employer**.

- Child tax credit is paid by the **Inland Revenue** to the **main carer**.

KEY FACTS – CGT BASICS: QUESTIONS

- *Check that you can fill in the blanks in the statements below before you attempt any questions. If in doubt, you should go back to your BPP Study Text Chapter 5 and revise first.*

- Capital gains tax is payable at the rates of ....%, ...% and ....%.

- Losses are relieved against current year gains and any excess loss is then carried ....

- Indexation allowance cannot create or increase a ....

- Indexation allowance can only be computed up to .... for individuals and trustees, instead .... relief is available.

- The amount of taper relief depends on whether the asset is a .... or a .... and on the length of ownership of the asset.

- An additional year of taper relief is given if a .... asset was held at ....

- Maximum taper relief for non-business assets is given for .... years ownership.

- Maximum taper relief for business assets is given for .... years ownership.

- Special rules apply to assets acquired before 31 March 1982. One computation is made based on .... and another based on .... If two gains arise, the .... gain is chargeable.

- If a disposal at a loss is made to a connected person, the loss can be used against gains arising in the same or future years to .... connected person.

- After acquisitions made on the same day, disposals of shares are next matched with shares acquired ....

- Share disposals matched with acquisitions made after 5 April 1998 are matched on a ....first out basis.

- The FA 1985 pool contains shares acquired between .... and ....

- The 1982 holding contains shares acquired between .... and ....

- Shares are business assets after 6 April 2000 in non-trading companies if the individual shareholder is an .... or .... of the company and does not have a .... in the company.

- Shares are business assets after 6 April 2000 in trading companies if the individual shareholder is an .... or .... of the company or the company is .... or the individual shareholder holds more than .... % of the voting rights.

KEY FACTS - CGT BASICS: ANSWERS

- *Could you fill in the blanks? The answers are in bold. Use this page for revision purposes as you approach the exam.*

- Capital gains tax is payable at the rates of **10%**, **20%** and **40%**.

- Losses are relieved against current year gains and any excess loss is then carried **forward**.

- Indexation allowance cannot create or increase a **loss**.

- Indexation allowance can only be computed up to **April 1998** for individuals and trustees, instead **taper** relief is available.

- The amount of taper relief depends on whether the asset is a **business asset** or a **non-business asset** and on the length of ownership of the asset.

- An additional year of taper relief is given if a **non-business** asset was held at **17 March 1998**.

- Maximum taper relief for non-business assets is given for **ten** years ownership.

- Maximum taper relief for business assets is given for **two** years ownership.

- Special rules apply to assets acquired before 31 March 1982. One computation is made based on **cost** and another based on **31 March 1982 market value**. If two gains arise, the **lower** gain is chargeable.

- If a disposal at a loss is made to a connected person, the loss can be used against gains arising in the same or future years to **the same** connected person.

- After acquisitions made on the same day, disposals of shares are next matched with shares acquired **in the next 30 days**.

- Share disposals matched with acquisitions made after 5 April 1998 are matched on a **last in first out** basis.

- The FA 1985 pool contains shares acquired between **6 April 1982** and **5 April 1998**.

- The 1982 holding contains shares acquired between **6 April 1965** and **5 April 1982**.

- Shares are business assets after 6 April 2000 in non-trading companies if an individual shareholder is an **officer** or **employee** of the company and does not have a **material interest** in the company.

- Shares are business assets after 6 April 2000 in trading companies if the individual shareholder is an **officer** or **employee** of the company or the company is **unlisted** or the individual shareholder holds more than **5%** of the voting rights.

KEY FACTS – CGT RELIEFS: QUESTIONS

- *Check that you can fill in the blanks in the statements below before you attempt any questions. If in doubt, you should go back to your BPP Study Text Chapter 6 and revise first.*

- If an individual gives away a qualifying asset, the transferor and the transferee can jointly elect for the transferor's gain to be reduced to nil. This reduction is made .... taper relief is taken into account.

- The amount of gain that can be deferred under EIS reinvestment relief is broadly the lower of the amount .... and the amount ....

- Generally, if the investor becomes non-resident broadly within .... years of the issue of the shares, the gain deferred will become chargeable in the tax year ....

- Wasting chattels are those with a useful life of .... and are .... CGT.

- If non wasting chattels are sold for more than £6,000, any gain is limited to a maximum of .... x (............................. less £6,000).

- A gain arising from the sale of an individual's only or main residence is exempt from CGT. This exemption also includes grounds, usually of up to ....

- Where the property has only been occupied for part of the period of ownership, the proportion of the gain exempted is:

  Total gain x   period of .... since ....
  _____
                period of .... since ....

- An individual always has deemed occupation of his only or main residence for the last .... years of ownership.

- Where a taxpayer has more than one residence, he may elect for one to be regarded as his main residence by notice to the Inspector of Taxes within .... years of commencing ownership of the second residence.

- Lettings relief may be available to cover letting as a residential accommodation during a period which is not covered by the main relief, but only up to a maximum of £................... of gain.

- Rollover relief is available on the disposal of a business asset, to defer the gain arising. Full relief is given if an amount equal to .... is invested in a new business asset.

- The new asset must be acquired within the period of .... before and .... after the disposal of the old asset to qualify for rollover relief.

KEY FACTS - CGT RELIEFS: ANSWERS

- *Could you fill in the blanks? The answers are in bold. Use this page for revision purposes as you approach the exam.*

- If an individual gives away a qualifying asset, the transferor and the transferee can jointly elect for the transferor's gain to be reduced to nil. This reduction is made **before** taper relief is taken into account.

- The amount of gain that can be deferred under EIS reinvestment relief is broadly the lower of the amount **subscribed by the investor for his shares** and the amount **specified in the claim**.

- Generally, if the investor becomes non-resident broadly within **three** years of the issue of the shares, the gain deferred will become chargeable in the tax year **of emigration**.

- Wasting chattels are those with a useful life of **50 years or less** and are **exempt from** CGT.

- If non wasting chattels are sold for more than £6,000, any gain is limited to a maximum of **5/3** x (**gross proceeds** less £6,000).

- A gain arising from the sale of an individual's only or main residence is exempt from CGT. This exemption also includes grounds, usually of up to **half a hectare**.

- Where the property has only been occupied for part of the period of ownership, the proportion of the gain exempted is:

    Total gain x   period of **occupation** since **1 April 1982**
                   period of **ownership** since **1 April 1982**

- An individual always has deemed occupation of his only or main residence for the last **three** years of ownership.

- Where a taxpayer has more than one residence, he may elect for one to be regarded as his main residence by notice to the Inspector of Taxes within **two** years of commencing ownership of the second residence.

- Lettings relief may be available to cover letting as a residential accommodation during a period which is not covered by the main relief, but only up to a maximum of **£40,000** of gain.

- Rollover relief is available on the disposal of a business asset, to defer the gain arising. Full relief is given if an amount equal to **the whole of the proceeds of the old asset** is invested in a new business asset.

- The new asset must be acquired within the period of **one year** before and **three years** after the disposal of the old asset to qualify for rollover relief.

KEY FACTS – OVERSEAS ASPECTS OF PERSONAL TAXATION: QUESTIONS

- *Check that you can fill in the blanks in the statements below before you attempt any questions. If in doubt, you should go back to your BPP Study Text Chapter 7 and revise first.*

- A person is resident in the UK if he is present in the UK for ……….. days or more (days of arrival and departure are ………………..) or if he makes substantial annual visits to the UK.

- A person whose home has previously been abroad and who comes to the UK to take up permanent residence or with the intention of staying for at least ……………… years, is regarded as resident and ordinarily resident from ……………………………

- If a person goes abroad for full-time service under a contract of employment such that his absence from the UK is for a period which includes …………………………………… and interim visits to the UK do not amount to ………………………….. or more in any tax year, he is normally regarded as not resident and not ordinarily resident for ……………………………..

- A person acquires a domicile of ……………… at birth, usually being the domicile of his ………………….

- Generally, a non-UK resident is liable to UK income tax only on income …………………………

- An individual who is UK resident but who is not domiciled in the UK, is liable to UK tax on overseas income on a ………………………….. only.

- Rental income from overseas property is taxed under ……………………………..

- Unilateral double taxation relief gives tax relief of the …………………… of UK tax on the foreign income and the foreign tax on the foreign income.

- Generally, a non-UK resident and non-UK ordinarily resident is …………………………. to UK capital gains tax on UK assets.

- Individuals who have acquired assets before they leave the UK will remain chargeable to UK CGT on those assets if they remain abroad for less than ……………….. tax years.

KEY FACTS - OVERSEAS ASPECTS OF PERSONAL TAXATION: ANSWERS

- *Could you fill in the blanks? The answers are in bold. Use this page for revision purposes as you approach the exam.*

- A person is resident in the UK if he is present in the UK for **183** days or more (days of arrival and departure are **excluded**) or if he makes substantial annual visits to the UK.

- A person whose home has previously been abroad and who comes to the UK to take up permanent residence or with the intention of staying for at least **three** years, is regarded as resident and ordinarily resident from **the date of his arrival**.

- If a person goes abroad for full-time service under a contract of employment such that his absence from the UK is for a period which includes **a complete tax year** and interim visits to the UK do not amount to **six months** or more in any tax year, he is normally regarded as not resident and not ordinarily resident for **the whole period of the contract**.

- A person acquires a domicile of **origin** at birth, usually being the domicile of his **father**.

- Generally, a non-UK resident is liable to UK income tax only on income **arising in the UK**.

- An individual who is UK resident but who is not domiciled in the UK, is liable to UK tax on overseas income on a **remittance basis** only.

- Rental income from overseas property is taxed under **Schedule D Case V**.

- Unilateral double taxation relief gives tax relief of the **lower** of UK tax on the foreign income and the foreign tax on the foreign income.

- Generally, a non-UK resident and non-UK ordinarily resident is **not chargeable** to UK capital gains tax on UK assets.

- Individuals who have acquired assets before they leave the UK will remain chargeable to UK CGT on those assets if they remain abroad for less than **five** tax years.

KEY FACTS – INHERITANCE TAX BASICS: QUESTIONS

- *Check that you can fill in the blanks in the statements below before you attempt any questions. If in doubt, you should go back to your BPP Study Text Chapters 8 and 9 and revise first.*

- The measure of a gift for inheritance tax is always..........................to the donor, not the ....by the donee.

- IHT is charged only where there is .... intent.

- All transfers of world-wide assets made by persons who are..........................in the UK are within the charge to IHT.

- Transfers between spouses (........................... living together) are exempt.

- A lifetime transfer made by one individual to another individual (other than spouse) is a .... transfer.

- If the donor of a chargeable lifetime transfer agrees to pay the tax on the transfer, the transfer must be ....

- When working out death tax on a lifetime transfer, it is necessary to look back .... years from the .... in order to work out the remaining nil rate band available.

- In order for Business Property Relief to apply to a transfer, it is usually necessary for the donor to have owned the gifted property as business property for at least .... years.

- The usual percentage reduction in value for land qualifying for agricultural property relief is .... %.

- Quick succession relief is available where there are successive charges to IHT within a .... year period.

- Reasonable funeral expenses may be deducted from the death estate. This .... the cost of a tombstone.

KEY FACTS - INHERITANCE TAX BASICS: ANSWERS

- *Could you fill in the blanks? The answers are in bold. Use this page for revision purposes as you approach the exam.*

- The measure of a gift for inheritance tax is always **the loss** to the donor, not the **amount gained** by the donee.

- IHT is charged only where there is **gratuitous** intent.

- All transfers of world-wide assets made by persons who are **domiciled** in the UK are within the charge to IHT.

- Transfers between spouses (**whether or not** living together) are exempt.

- A lifetime transfer made by one individual to another individual (other than spouse) is a **potentially exempt** transfer.

- If the donor of a chargeable lifetime transfer agrees to pay the tax on the transfer, the transfer must be **grossed up**.

- When working out death tax on a lifetime transfer, it is necessary to look back **seven** years from the **transfer** in order to work out the remaining nil rate band available.

- In order for Business Property Relief to apply to a transfer, it is usually necessary for the donor to have owned the gifted property as business property for at least **two** years.

- The usual percentage reduction in value for land qualifying for agricultural property relief is **100**%.

- Quick succession relief is available where there are successive charges to IHT within a **five** year period.

- Reasonable funeral expenses may be deducted from the death estate. This **includes** the cost of a tombstone.

KEY FACTS – INHERITANCE TAX ADDITIONAL ASPECTS: QUESTIONS

- *Check that you can fill in the blanks in the statements below before you attempt any questions. If in doubt, you should go back to your BPP Study Text Chapter 10 and revise first.*

- An individual gifts his house to his son, but continues to live there rent-free. This is a gift……………………………….., so that if the individual dies, the house is treated as being ……………………………… at its value at the date …………………………..

- Property can be owned jointly as joint tenants so that the property eventually becomes owned by……………………… or as tenants in common where the joint owner's share passes on death by ………………………………………

- Where husband and wife make wills, it is usual to insert a …………………………………… which provides that a gift to the other spouse should only take effect if the spouse survives a certain length of time, typically thirty days.

- If a discretionary trust is made in a will and an appointment is made within three months after the death and ………………….. years after the death, there will be no ……………………….. charge to IHT.

- No one can be forced to accept property passing under a will, intestacy or joint tenancy. It is possible to …………………………….. such an entitlement.

- If a disclaimer is made in writing for no consideration within …………………. years of the deceased owner's death, for IHT purposes the original beneficiary is not treated as making a…………………………….. The property is treated as passing as if the deceased had made a will providing for the disposition to ……………………………………………

- In order for a variation to be treated in the same way as an disclaimer, the variation must include …………………………..

- The settlor of a trust set up under a variation will be the ……………………….. for the purposes of IHT and the ………………………….. for the purposes of CGT and income tax.

- The latest date for the submission of an account of the death estate by the personal representatives is ……………………….. following the end of the month of death.

- IHT on chargeable lifetime transfers is due on the later of …………………………………… and ……………………………after the end of the month of transfer.

- IHT can be paid by …………………………… instalments on certain property such as land and buildings.

- If property on which payment by instalments has been claimed is sold then ……………………………………………………………….. must then be paid.

KEY FACTS - INHERITANCE TAX ADDITIONAL ASPECTS: ANSWERS

- *Could you fill in the blanks? The answers are in bold. Use this page for revision purposes as you approach the exam.*

- An individual gifts his house to his son, but continues to live there rent-free. This is a gift **with reservation of benefit** so that if the individual dies, the house is treated as being **in his death estate** at its value at the date **of death**.

- Property can be owned jointly as joint tenants so that the property eventually becomes owned by **the sole survivor** or as tenants in common where the joint owner's share passes on death by **will or intestacy**.

- Where husband and wife make wills, it is usual to insert a **survivorship clause** which provides that a gift to the other spouse should only take effect if the spouse survives a certain length of time, typically thirty days.

- If a discretionary trust is made in a will and an appointment is made within three months after the death and **two** years after the death, there will be no **exit** charge to IHT.

- No one can be forced to accept property passing under a will, intestacy or joint tenancy. It is possible to **disclaim** such an entitlement.

- If a disclaimer is made in writing for no consideration within **two** years of the deceased owner's death, for IHT purposes the original beneficiary is not treated as making a **transfer of value.** The property is treated as passing as if the deceased had made a will providing for the disposition to **the person who receives the property as a result of the disclaimer**.

- In order for a variation to be treated in the same way as a disclaimer, the variation must include **a statement to that effect**.

- The settlor of a trust set up under a variation will be the **deceased** for the purposes of IHT and the **original beneficiary** for the purposes of CGT and income tax.

- The latest date for the submission of an account of the death estate by the personal representatives is **twelve months** following the end of the month of death.

- IHT on chargeable lifetime transfers is due on the later of **30 April in the following tax year** and **six months** after the end of the month of transfer.

- IHT can be paid by **ten equal annual** instalments on certain property such as land and buildings.

- If property on which payment by instalments has been claimed is sold then **all the outstanding tax** must then be paid.

KEY FACTS – TAXATION OF INVESTMENTS: QUESTIONS

- *Check that you can fill in the blanks in the statements below before you attempt any questions. If in doubt, you should go back to your BPP Study Text Chapter 11 and revise first.*

- The first £...... of interest from a National Savings Ordinary account is free of income tax for individuals.

- Interest received from National Savings Fixed-rate and Index-linked Certificates is .... income tax.

- Where a gilt is purchased after 5 April 1998, interest is automatically paid ...., unless the holder elects to receive it ....

- Individuals who invest in shares under the Enterprise Investment Scheme (EIS) can claim a tax reducer of ....% of the amount subscribed, up to a limit of £............ per tax year.

- EIS relief can be claimed by an individual who subscribes wholly .... for .... in a qualifying company.

- If shares acquired under the EIS scheme are disposed of at least .... years after acquisition, any gain is exempt from CGT.

- Dividends on ordinary shares in a Venture Capital Trust (VCT) are .... income, subject to a limit of .... of investment per tax year.

- Under an occupational pension scheme, an employee may make contributions up to ...., subject to the earnings cap.

- Under a personal pension scheme, an election can be made for any contribution to be treated as paid in the previous tax year if the premium is paid by ....and the election is made ....

- The basis year for net relevant earnings can be the year in which the contribution is made or any of the previous .... tax years.

- Benefits under a personal pension scheme can be taken from the age of .... and must begin at .... at the latest.

- In order for a payout from a qualifying life assurance policy to be tax-free, the premiums on the policy must be paid for a minimum of the life of ...., ... years or .... of the term.

- Under a non-qualifying policy, up to ....% per policy year may be withdrawn with no immediate tax implications.

- Profits on the encashment of units or shares in offshore non-distributor funds are subject to .... tax, not .... tax.

- The premium taxed under Schedule A on a lease premium is the whole premium less ....% for each .... year of the lease except the ....

- The maximum investment under an Individual Savings Account (ISA) is £................... .

KEY FACTS - TAXATION OF INVESTMENTS: ANSWERS

- *Could you fill in the blanks? The answers are in bold. Use this page for revision purposes as you approach the exam.*

- The first £**70** of interest from a National Savings Ordinary account is free of income tax for individuals.

- Interest received from National Savings Fixed-rate and Index-linked Certificates is **free of** income tax.

- Where a gilt is purchased after 5 April 1998, interest is automatically paid **gross**, unless the holder elects to receive it **net of 20% income tax**.

- Individuals who invest in shares under the Enterprise Investment Scheme (EIS) can claim a tax reducer of **20**% of the amount subscribed, up to a limit of £**200,000** per tax year.

- EIS relief can be claimed by an individual who subscribes wholly **in cash** for **new ordinary shares** in a qualifying company.

- If shares acquired under the EIS scheme are disposed of at least **three** years after acquisition, any gain is exempt from CGT.

- Dividends on ordinary shares in a Venture Capital Trust (VCT) are **tax-free** income, subject to a limit of £**200,000** of investment per tax year.

- Under an occupational pension scheme, an employee may make contributions up to **15% of his gross emoluments**, subject to the earnings cap.

- Under a personal pension scheme, an election can be made for any contribution to be treated as paid in the previous tax year if the premium is paid by **31 January following the end of the tax year in which the contribution is to be treated as having been made** and the election is made **at or before the time the payment is made**.

- The basis year for net relevant earnings can be the year in which the contribution is made or any of the previous **five** tax years.

- Benefits under a personal pension scheme can be taken from the age of **50** and must begin at **75** at the latest.

- In order for a payout from a qualifying life assurance policy to be tax-free, the premiums on the policy must be paid for a minimum of the life of **the life assured**, **10** years or **three-quarters** of the term.

- Under a non-qualifying policy, up to **5**% per policy year may be withdrawn with no immediate tax implications.

- Profits on the encashment of units or shares in offshore non-distributor funds are subject to **income** tax, not **capital gains** tax.

- The premium taxed under Schedule A on a lease premium is the whole premium less **2**% for each **complete** year of the lease except the **first year**.

- The maximum investment under an Individual Savings Account (ISA) is £**7,000**.

KEY FACTS – ESSENTIALS OF TRUSTS AND TRUSTEES: QUESTIONS

- *Check that you can fill in the blanks in the statements below before you attempt any questions. If in doubt, you should go back to your BPP Study Text Chapters 12 and 13 and revise first.*

- Trusts are an invention of the law of ……………...

- The individuals who have control over trust property are called …………………... and those individuals who can benefit from the trust property are called ………………………...

- Chattels personal are divided into two sub-groups which are ……………………………… such as life policies and shares and …………………………………… such as cash, furniture and books.

- The three certainties required for a valid trust are certainty of ……………..., certainty of ……………… and certainty of ……………………...

- Under s.36(1) Trustee Act 1925, persons who can appoint new trustees are first ……………………………….. or, if none, ……………………………………… or, if none, ………………………………………...

- Trustees can be discharged from their duties by ……………… or ………………… or ………………… or ………………………...

- A trustee who is in breach of trust is usually …………………………… for the loss.

- S.31 Trustee Act 1925 provides that income must be paid to beneficiaries once they have attained ………………………… (……. years) unless the trust instrument provides otherwise.

- S.32 Trustee Act 1925 gives the trustees power to pay out capital to a beneficiary before the trust states that they will become absolutely entitled to it, but only up to ………….. of the capital, unless the trust states otherwise.

- S.3 Trustee Act 2000 gives a power to trustees to make …………………………..

- A trustee has a duty to convert (that is, ……………………………………………………….), where the trust requires it, statute requires it or under the rule in *Howe v Dartmouth*.

- In general, a trustee in bankruptcy may recover assets placed into trust, except those settled under the …………………………………….

BPP PROFESSIONAL EDUCATION

KEY FACTS - ESSENTIALS OF TRUSTS AND TRUSTEES: ANSWERS

- *Could you fill in the blanks? The answers are in bold. Use this page for revision purposes as you approach the exam.*

- Trusts are an invention of the law of **equity**.

- The individuals who have control over trust property are called **trustees** and those individuals who can benefit from the trust property are called **beneficiaries**.

- Chattels personal are divided into two sub-groups which are **choses in action** such as life policies and shares and **choses in possession** such as cash, furniture and books.

- The three certainties required for a valid trust are certainty of **words**, certainty of **subject** and certainty of **objects**.

- Under s.36(1) Trustee Act 1925, persons who can appoint new trustees are first **those nominated in the trust instrument** or, if none, **the surviving trustees** or, if none, **the personal representatives of the longest surviving trustee.**

- Trustees can be discharged from their duties by **disclaimer** or **death** or **retirement** or **removal**.

- A trustee who is in breach of trust is usually **sued personally** for the loss.

- S.31 Trustee Act 1925 provides that income must be paid to beneficiaries once they have attained **their majority** (**18** years) unless the trust instrument provides otherwise.

- S.32 Trustee Act 1925 gives the trustees power to pay out capital to a beneficiary before the trust states that they will become absolutely entitled to it, but only up to **half** of the capital, unless the trust states otherwise.

- S.3 Trustee Act 2000 gives a power to trustees to make **any kind of investment that they could make if they were absolutely entitled to the assets of the trust**.

- A trustee has a duty to convert (that is, **sell some assets and invest in other assets**), where the trust requires it, statute requires it or under the rule in *Howe v Dartmouth*.

- In general, a trustee in bankruptcy may recover assets placed into trust, except those settled under the **Married Woman's Property Act 1882**.

KEY FACTS – STATUTORY AND NON-STATUTORY TRUSTS: QUESTIONS

- *Check that you can fill in the blanks in the statements below before you attempt any questions. If in doubt, you should go back to your BPP Study Text Chapters 14 and 15 and revise first.*

- ………………… trusts are trusts which are created by virtue of an Act of Parliament, for example the property of a person dying without a will (……………..) vests in his personal representatives on trust.

- The Married Women's Property Act (MWPA) 1882 enables life assurance policies to be written under a statutory trust for the benefit of ………………………………...

- A policy written under the MWPA must be a policy of assurance on ………………...

- The rule against perpetuities states that the grant of a contingent interest will be void unless it vests within the perpetuity period. In modern trusts, this period is often expressly stated to be one of ………………. years or less.

- For a will trust where all the beneficiaries are aged at least eighteen years, the maximum accumulation period, during which income can be accumulated rather than paid out to beneficiaries, is the period of …………………… years from the death of the settlor.

- An implied trust may arise where one person ………………………………… to another person but retains an interest in it, such as where property is purchased in …………………………of another or the property is not …………………….. to the beneficiaries.

- A trust which is created by law to protect the interests and rights of an individual which are affected by the actions of another individual are called ………………………… trusts.

KEY FACTS - STATUTORY AND NON-STATUTORY TRUSTS: ANSWERS

- *Could you fill in the blanks? The answers are in bold. Use this page for revision purposes as you approach the exam.*

- **Statutory** trusts are trusts which are created by virtue of an Act of Parliament, for example the property of a person dying without a will (**intestate**) vests in his personal representatives on trust.

- The Married Women's Property Act (MWPA) 1882 enables life assurance policies to be written under a statutory trust for the benefit of **the assured's spouse and/or children**.

- A policy written under the MWPA must be a policy of assurance on **own life**.

- The rule against perpetuities states that the grant of a contingent interest will be void unless it vests within the perpetuity period. In modern trusts, this period is often expressly stated to be one of **80** years or less.

- For a will trust where all the beneficiaries are aged at least eighteen years, the maximum accumulation period, during which income can be accumulated rather than paid out to beneficiaries, is the period of **21** years from the death of the settlor.

- An implied trust may arise where one person **transfers property** to another person but retains an interest in it, such as where property is purchased in **the name** of another or the property is not **fully transferred** to the beneficiaries.

- A trust which is created by law to protect the interests and rights of an individual which are affected by the actions of another individual are called **constructive** trusts.

KEY FACTS – TAXATION OF TRUSTS AND USES OF TRUSTS: QUESTIONS

- *Check that you can fill in the blanks in the statements below before you attempt any questions. If in doubt, you should go back to your BPP Study Text Chapters 16 and 17 and revise first.*

- In a trust with an interest in possession, some beneficiaries are entitled to ……………………… from the trust assets as it arises.

- Trustees of an interest in possession trust are taxable at 22% on ……………………… income, 20% on …………………………… income and 10% on ……………………… income.

- Trustees of a discretionary trust pay tax on income available for distribution at …………………% on non-dividend income and ………………% on dividend income.

- Any payments of income to a beneficiary of a discretionary trust are made net of tax of ………………% and are ……………………… income of the beneficiary.

- The income of a bare trust created by a parent for a minor child is taxed on the ……………………, subject to a de minimis amount of £………… per tax year.

- Trustees are entitled to an annual exemption for CGT which is ………………… of that given to an individual and pay CGT at the rate of ……………%.

- When a beneficiary with an interest in possession dies, there is a disposal by the trustees of the trust assets at market value. However, any gain made by the trustees is ……………………, unless ……………………… was claimed on the creation of the trust, in which case only the amount of the gain up to the ………………………… is chargeable.

- If assets leave an accumulation and maintenance trust, for example, when a beneficiary attains specified age and becomes entitled to capital, gift relief on all types of asset is only available if the beneficiary has not already been entitled to ……………………… those assets.

- There is an IHT charge on discretionary trust property at least every ……………… years from the commencement of the trust. If property ceases to be held on discretionary trusts in between times there is an ……………………… charge.

- An accumulation and maintenance trust is a type of discretionary trust where at least one of the beneficiaries becomes entitled to at least the right to income of the trust by a specified age not exceeding the age of ………………………

- A nil rate band discretionary trust in a will uses the nil rate band of the deceased, but allows the surviving spouse to benefit from the trust assets, without it forming part of …………………………………

- Under a flexible power of appointment trust, there are two classes of beneficiary: ……………………… beneficiaries will receive the policy proceeds in the absence of any alternative appointment by the assured and ……………………… beneficiaries whom the assured can select to receive benefits.

- The creation of a flexible power of appointment trust is usually a ……………………… transfer for IHT purposes.

- Regular premiums paid by the assured may be exempt from IHT either because they are covered by the ……………exemption or the ……………………………… exemption.

KEY FACTS - TAXATION OF TRUSTS AND USES OF TRUSTS: ANSWERS

- *Could you fill in the blanks? The answers are in bold. Use this page for revision purposes as you approach the exam.*

- In a trust with an interest in possession, some beneficiaries are entitled to **income** from the trust assets as it arises.

- Trustees of an interest in possession trust are taxable at 22% on **non-savings** income, 20% on **savings (excluding dividends)** income and 10% on **dividend** income.

- Trustees of a discretionary trust pay tax on income available for distribution at **40%** on non-dividend income and **32.5%** on dividend income.

- Any payments of income to a beneficiary of a discretionary trust are made net of tax of **40%** and are **non-savings** income of the beneficiary.

- The income of a bare trust created by a parent for a minor child is taxed on the **parent**, subject to a de minimis amount of **£100** per tax year.

- Trustees are entitled to an annual exemption for CGT which is **half** of that given to an individual and pay CGT at the rate of **40%**.

- When a beneficiary with an interest in possession dies, there is a disposal by the trustees of the trust assets at market value. However, any gain made by the trustees is **exempt**, unless **gift relief** was claimed on the creation of the trust, in which case only the amount of the gain up to the **amount of the gift relief** is chargeable.

- If assets leave an accumulation and maintenance trust, for example, when a beneficiary attains specified age and becomes entitled to capital, gift relief on all types of asset is only available if the beneficiary has not already been entitled to **the income of** those assets.

- There is an IHT charge on discretionary trust property at least every **ten** years from the commencement of the trust. If property ceases to be held on discretionary trusts in between times there is an **exit** charge.

- An accumulation and maintenance trust is a type of discretionary trust where at least one of the beneficiaries becomes entitled to at least the right to income of the trust by a specified age not exceeding the age of **25**.

- A nil rate band discretionary trust in a will uses the nil rate band of the deceased, but allows the surviving spouse to benefit from the trust assets, without it forming part of **the surviving spouse's estate**.

- Under a flexible power of appointment trust, there are two classes of beneficiary: **default** beneficiaries will receive the policy proceeds in the absence of any alternative appointment by the assured and **discretionary** beneficiaries whom the assured can select to receive benefits.

- The creation of a flexible power of appointment trust is usually a **potentially exempt** transfer for IHT purposes.

- Regular premiums paid by the assured may be exempt from IHT either because they are covered by the **annual** exemption or the **regular gifts out of income** exemption.

KEY FACTS – PENSIONS, UNIT TRUSTS, BANKRUPTCY AND POWERS OF ATTORNEY: QUESTIONS

- *Check that you can fill in the blanks in the statements below before you attempt any questions. If in doubt, you should go back to your BPP Study Text Chapters 18 and 19 and revise first.*

- Occupational pension trusts can be established by .... or by .... or by .... or by ....

- Personal pensions can be established under trust by using a .... trust or by an .... trust.

- Writing a death benefit in trust has two benefits. First the beneficiaries can receive the money immediately without waiting for a .... Second, the benefit passes free of ....

- The assets of a unit trust are held by ....

- The marketing and management of a unit trust is carried out by the unit trust ....

- Income equalisation is the refund of capital following the purchase of units to represent the income accrued before ....

- Expenses connected with unit trusts include an .... charge, an .... charge and an .... charge.

- A court will not entertain a bankruptcy petition from a creditor unless he is owed at least £............... on an unsecured debt.

- When a bankruptcy order has been made, the .... as interim receiver takes control of the debtor's assets, until a .... has been appointed.

- As a general rule, after an individual has been declared bankrupt, a .... creditor retains his rights in respect of any property over which he has a valid charge.

- The debts of a bankrupt person must be paid in the following order: the costs of ...., ... debts and debts owed to .... creditors.

- A bankruptcy order is normally discharged .... years after the date of the order.

- A power of attorney is a document made by the donor which gives the donee power to ....

- A power of attorney will cease to have effect if the donor becomes mentally incapable unless it is an .... power of attorney.

KEY FACTS - PENSIONS, UNIT TRUSTS, BANKRUPTCY AND POWERS OF ATTORNEY: ANSWERS

- *Could you fill in the blanks? The answers are in bold. Use this page for revision purposes as you approach the exam.*

- Occupational pension trusts can be established by **exchange of letters** or by **trust deed** or by **declaration of trust** or by **board resolution**.

- Personal pensions can be established under trust by using a **master** trust or by an **individual** trust.

- Writing a death benefit in trust has two benefits. First the beneficiaries can receive the money immediately without waiting for a **grant of representation**. Second, the benefit passes free of **inheritance tax**.

- The assets of a unit trust are held by **independent trustees**.

- The marketing and management of a unit trust is carried out by the unit trust **manager**.

- Income equalisation is the refund of capital following the purchase of units to represent the income accrued before **the date of purchase**.

- Expenses connected with unit trusts include an **initial** charge, an **annual management** charge and an **exit** charge.

- A court will not entertain a bankruptcy petition from a creditor unless he is owed at least £**750** on an unsecured debt.

- When a bankruptcy order has been made, the **Official Receiver** as interim receiver takes control of the debtor's assets, until a **trustee in bankruptcy** has been appointed.

- As a general rule, after an individual has been declared bankrupt, a **secured** creditor retains his rights in respect of any property over which he has a valid charge.

- The debts of a bankrupt person must be paid in the following order: the costs of **the bankruptcy**, **preferential** debts and debts owed to **ordinary unsecured** creditors.

- A bankruptcy order is normally discharged **three** years after the date of the order.

- A power of attorney is a document made by the donor which gives the donee power to **act for the donor in legal matters**.

- A power of attorney will cease to have effect if the donor becomes mentally incapable unless it is an **enduring** power of attorney.

1 **HARRY**

Harry has the following income for 2004/05:
- salary £30,000
- building society interest received £1,800
- dividends received £4,000

He is single. Calculate his tax liability. **(8 marks)**

2 **TAX CREDIT**

Elizabeth is a widow with one child aged 2. Elizabeth earns £16,000 in 2004/05 and has no other income. She works 35 hours per week but does not pay child care.

Show the amount of Child Tax Credit and Working Tax Credit available to her for 2004/05.

(8 marks)

3 **GIFT AID**

Mr Cummings, aged 35, earned a salary of £45,000 in 2004/05. On 1 October 2004 he made a gift aid payment to Oxfam of £5,460 (net). He has no other source of income.

How much income tax remains payable if he paid £8,576 of tax via the PAYE system?

(7 marks)

4 **BILL SMITH**

In the tax year 2004/05 Bill Smith, aged 68 and a widower, received a total gross income of £19,200 from pensions. Calculate his income tax liability for that year. **(7 marks)**

5 **ACCOMMODATION**

Ralph has the use of a house belonging to his employer, for which he pays a notional rent of £2,500. The annual rateable value is £3,000. Ralph has lived in the house since October 2000. It had cost the company £175,000 in October 1999.

The official rate at the start of 2004/05 was 5%.

Calculate the assessable benefit for 2004/05 assuming that the accommodation is not 'job-related'. **(3 marks)**

6 **CAR AND FUEL BENEFIT**

Stuart Revver has the use of a car provided by his employer. The car had a list price of £14,000. The employer also pays all running costs, including petrol.

(a) Calculate his assessable car benefit for 2004/05 if the CO_2 emission figure is:

    (i)   147g/km; or **(1 mark)**
    (ii)   157g/km **(1 mark)**

(b) Calculate his assessable fuel benefit for 2004/05 in each case. **(2 marks)**

(c) Calculate Stuart's car and fuel benefit if he only had the use of the car in (a)(i) for 6 months in 2004/05. **(2 marks)**

(Total marks available: 6)

7   **MR TYE**

Mr Tye is an employee of Taverner plc.

	£
Salary for 2004/05	15,000
Bonus for y/e 31.12.03 (received 30.6.04)	7,000
Bonus for y/e 31.12.04 (received 30.6.05)	6,500

The bonus is approved each year at the AGM of the company in May.

(a)   What are his Class 1 Primary NIC's for 2004/05 assuming he receives his salary weekly? He is contracted into the state second pension.   (4 marks)

(b)   Assuming in the previous example Mr Tye had been a director, calculate his Primary Class 1 NIC's for 2004/05.   (2 marks)

(Total marks available: 6)

8   **CLASS 2 NICs**

Describe Class 2 NIC contributions.   **(4 marks)**

9   **JOE JOSEPH**

In the tax year 2004/05 Joe Joseph realised a net capital gain (after indexation allowance and taper relief) of £13,000 from the sale of shares. His total taxable income for that year was £26,800. Calculate the capital gains tax paid.   **(5 marks)**

10   **LOSSES**

Jim made disposals of assets during 2004/05 resulting in gains of £13,000 and losses of £3,000. None of the assets were entitled to taper relief. He had unrelieved losses brought forward of £6,000.

What is his loss left unrelieved at the end of 2004/05?   **(3 marks)**

11   **PATRICK**

On 1 May 2004 Patrick sold a freehold shop used for his business as a greengrocer, for £225,000. He bought the shop on 10 January 2003, paying £185,364.

Calculate the chargeable gain arising on the sale.   **(4 marks)**

12   **CONSTANT**

Constant Lambert purchased the following holdings in Rio Grande plc:

> January 1985   1,000 shares for £5,000 (Indexed cost @ April 1998 £8,715)
> February 2001 1,000 shares for £4,000

In May 2004 he sold 2,000 shares for £14,000.

Calculate the gain on disposal of the shares before taper relief.   **(6 marks)**

13   **MAXWELL**

Maxwell bought a workshop used in his trade on 1.4.82 for £75,000. He gave it to his son on 1.1.05 when its market value was £210,000.

Indexed rise: 1.047

(a) Calculate the chargeable gain on disposal of the workshop and the new base cost of the asset if:

    (i) no gift relief claim is made. (3 marks)

    (ii) such a claim is made. (1 mark)

(b) Recalculate these figures assuming that his son actually paid him £95,000 for the workshop and a gift relief claim is made. (3 marks)

(Total marks available: 7)

14   JACOB

Jacob sold an antique painting on 30 July 2004 for £200,000, realising a chargeable gain of £80,000. He acquired the painting in May 2001. He subscribed for an 8% stake in an EIS issue by Esau Ltd on 30 September 2003 for £95,000. There were no other capital transactions in 2004/05. Determine the optimum position for Jacob. **(3 marks)**

15   GLENDA

Glenda works partly in the UK and partly abroad, but does not qualify for exemption on her foreign earnings. Her income in 2004/05 is as follows:

Schedule E: UK duties   £25,815

                  Foreign duties £12,000 gross (foreign tax suffered = £4,400)

Interest income (gross)   £1,525

Calculate Glenda's total UK tax liability for 2004/05. **(7 marks)**

16   RESIDENCE

Briefly explain when an individual who is neither UK resident nor ordinarily resident can be liable to UK CGT. **(7 marks)**

17   MR ARM

Mr Arm made the following gifts during his lifetime:

		£
13 May 2001	Gift to daughter	155,000
23 August 2001	Gift into discretionary trust	243,000

He died on 7 June 2004 leaving a death estate valued at £400,000. Everything was left to his wife.

Nil rate band 2001/02 = £242,000.

Calculate any IHT payable during life and on death, asuming Mr Arm pays any lifetime tax due. **(7 marks)**

18   HENRY

Henry died on 30 November 2004, owning 3,200 shares in Henry Ltd and unquoted company. This represented 16% of the company's share capital and was worth £100,000.

The company's net assets at that date were:

	£
Freehold	400,000
Plant and machinery	80,000
Goodwill	150,000
Investments	170,000
Net current assets	200,000
	1,000,000

Show the valuation of the shares in his estate. **(3 marks)**

19   MR L

Mr K transferred shares to Mr L on his death on 4 March 2000. The chargeable (ie gross) value of the transfer was £48,531 including IHT of £8,420 paid by Mr K's estate. On 8 May 2004 Mr L died leaving a chargeable estate valued at £327,000. He had made no lifetime transfers.

Show the tax liability on Mr L's estate. **(4 marks)**

QSR percentages

Time between IHT charges	%
Less than 1 year	100
1-2 years	80
2-3 years	60
3-4 years	40
4-5 years	20

20   TAPER RELIEF

When does taper relief for inheritance tax apply and who can potentially benefit from taper relief? **(5 marks)**

21   CUTHBERT

Explain the inheritance tax implications of the following gifts ignoring the £3,000 annual exemption. These gifts were made in 2004/05 and are the only gifts made by the donor in the last seven years.

(a)   Cuthbert gave £250 each to his twenty best pals at the golf club.

(2 marks)

(b)   He gave £50,000 to an accumulation and maintenance trust set up for the benefit of his grandchildren. **(4 marks)**

(c)   He gave £300,000 to a discretionary trust set up for the benefit of his children.

(6 marks)
(Total marks available: 12)

22   GILES

Giles owns a farm which he wishes to pass to his son.

Outline the time limits that need to be satisfied for the farm to qualify for agricultural property relief. **(4 marks)**

23   GREGORY

Gregory owns a house. He gifts it to his son, Ronald. Gregory continues to live in the house on his own without making any payment to Ronald, until his death two years later.

Explain how this arrangement will be charged to IHT. **(5 marks)**

24   DEATH ESTATE

Set out the conditions that need to be satisfied for a variation of a death estate to be treated as if the deceased had made a Will in the same terms as the terms of the variation. **(6 marks)**

25   JOHN

John took out a single premium policy on 31 October 1998 for £15,000. He withdrew 4% of the premium in each of the next five years and he encashed the policy on 30 June 2004 receiving £20,000. In the tax year 2004/05 his other income (all earnings) was £30,200 after deducting his personal allowance.

Calculate the amount of additional tax payable in respect of the bond. **(7 marks)**

26   ISA

Distinguish between a 'mini' individual savings account and a 'maxi' individual savings account and detail the limits applicable to each. Deal only with individual investors aged 18 or over. **(7 marks)**

27   PENELOPE

Penelope has just acquired a cottage in Wales which she intends to let out to holidaymakers.

State the conditions that must be fulfilled for the property to qualify as a furnished holiday letting. **(5 marks)**

28   MR TIPPETT

Mr Tippett was born in May 1962 and is self employed. Details for recent years are as follows:

	NRE
	£
1998/99	40,000
1999/00	38,000
2000/01	32,000
2001/02	35,000
2002/03	37,000
2003/04	25,000
2004/05	27,000

Explain what basis year should be used for pension contributions in 2004/05 and the maximum contribution that could be paid in that year. **(5 marks)**

29   ENTERPRISE INVESTMENT SCHEME

What are the tax advantages of investing in an Enterprise Investment Scheme? **(4 marks)**

30 URSULA

Ursula created an interest in possession trust in her will. The terms of the will did not exclude the trustees' duty to convert.

(a) Other than life assurance based investments, state three types of investment which the trustees would have a duty to convert to cash for reinvestment. Explain why the investments should be converted. (6 marks)

(b) State the period of time in which the trustees must convert such inappropriate trust assets. (2 marks)

(Total marks available: 8)

31 CERTAINTIES

What are the certainties required for a trust to be valid? (4 marks)

32 TRUSTEES

(a) List five persons who may appoint trustees. (5 marks)

(b) What is the maximum number of trustees for a trust of land? (1 mark)

(Total marks available: 6)

33 BENEFICIARIES

List two of the advantages and two of the disadvantages of using a trust set up under the Married Women's Property Act 1882 compared with using a non-statutory trust.

(4 marks)

34 LOUISA

Louisa and her husband Wesley have two children, Emma aged 18 and Sarah aged 9. Louisa and Wesley own their own house, valued at £160,000 (no mortgage) as joint tenants. They also jointly own a bank account with £10,000 in it, and Wesley has Stock Exchange investments worth £85,000. Wesley arranged life assurance on his life which is held by him and which will pay a death benefit of £300,000.

What would be the distribution of Wesley's estate if he were to die, without making a will?

(8 marks)

35 SALLY SMITH

The MWPA is a statutory trust which can apply to life policies.

Sally Smith is married to Harold. They have two children; Mark aged 6 and Julia aged 8.

(a) Outline the requirements which must be met if Mr and Mrs Smith wish to make use of the MWPA provisions. (4 marks)

(b) What protection does a MWPA trust afford in the event of the policyholder being made bankrupt? (2 marks)

(Total marks available: 6)

36   ACCUMULATION PERIODS

State the accumulation periods for a settlement as permitted by statute.   **(6 marks)**

37   TAX PLANNING

List the main tax planning considerations of a lifetime Bare Trust established by a parent for a minor child.   **(6 marks)**

38   G TRUST

The G trust is a discretionary trust. The following receipts/payments relate to the trust in 2004/05:

	£
Receipts:	
Rental income	5,900
Debenture interest received	2,320
Payments:	
On let property	780
Trustees expenses	300
Distribution (net)	
to H (a beneficiary)	1,000

Produce a statement of trust income for 2004/05, showing the amount of tax payable by self assessment. Also show the entries on the certificate of deduction of income tax that would be given to H.   **(7 marks)**

39   SETTLOR

A settlor is considering setting up a trust for his two children, aged 20 and 22. He does not want the children to have rights to capital, but would not mind them being entitled to income in a couple of years time. The assets to be settled are quoted shares (all holdings less than 5%) worth £200,000 with large gains attaching to the shares. He has not previously made any substantial gifts.

Explain what types of trust the settlor could set up to satisfy his requirements and outline the IHT and CGT consequences of setting up each type of trust.   **(6 marks)**

40   BILL

Bill is considering transferring some shares into a trust for the benefit of his family.

The beneficiaries will exclude both Bill and his wife.

The shares do not qualify for business property relief, nor are they classed as 'business assets'.

(a)   What distinguishes an interest in possession trust from a discretionary trust?

(3 marks)

(b)   Outline the potential tax consequences on Bill as settlor if he were to transfer the shares into an interest in possession trust.   (4 marks)

(c)   Outline the potential tax consequences on Bill as settlor if he were to transfer the shares into a discretionary trust.   (4 marks)

(Total marks available:11)

41   BARE TRUST

(a)   What is a bare trust and what are the specific duties of its trustees?   (2 marks)

(b)   Explain the tax treatment of income generated by a bare trust when the beneficiary is a minor and the settlor is a parent.   (3 marks)

(Total marks available: 5)

42   DEATH BENEFITS

List the potential advantages to members of an Occupational Pension Scheme and their dependants of the death benefits being set up under trust.   **(4 marks)**

43   VOLUNTARY ARRANGEMENT

Explain what is meant by an individual voluntary arrangement and the advantage of such an arrangement over a bankruptcy order.   **(5 marks)**

44   POWER OF ATTORNEY

(a)   Explain what is meant by a power of attorney.   (3 marks)

(b)   Describe the contents and execution of a general power of attorney under s10 Powers of Attorney Act 1971.   (3 marks)

(Total marks available: 6)

45   ELSIE

Elsie is aged 80 and currently in good mental health. However, she is concerned that she may become mentally incapable of managing her affairs in future and would like her daughter, Dorothy, to be able to take over in this case.

(a)   State what type of arrangement Elsie could set up now which would accord with her wishes.   (1 mark)

(b)   Explain what Dorothy would have to do if Elsie becomes mentally incapable and the extent to which she can manage Elsie's affairs.   (6 marks)

(Total marks available: 7)

46   MR K

Mr K is chairman and chief executive of Lyngstad Ltd.

He receives a salary of £43,484 per annum and during the income tax year 2004/05 he is provided with the following benefits.

The company provided him with the use of a 2.2 litre Jaguar motor car costing £20,000 from 6 April 2004. The CO_2 emission figure for the car was 210g/km. The car was used for private and business use.

On 31 July 2004 he was involved in a serious road accident and the car was written off. He was charged with dangerous driving and the company met his legal costs of £2,000.

When he resumed work on 1 October 2004, he was provided with a Mercedes car costing £30,000 and the use of a chauffeur. This car is used solely for business purposes. The CO_2 emissions figure is 265g/km.

While he had use of the Jaguar, he contributed 50% of the cost of his private petrol.

Throughout the year, his wife, who is not employed by the company, has been provided with the use of a 2 litre BMW car costing £15,000. The company meets all running costs including petrol. The CO_2 emissions figure is 215g/km.

He is provided with the use of two suits which had been purchased by the company at a cost of £800 in total.

Questions:

(a) Compute the total amount of benefits assessable on Mr K for the income tax year 2004/05.   (15 marks)

(b) Assuming Mr K also received dividends of £18,000 in the tax year, compute Mr K's total tax liability for 2004/05.   (20 marks)

(c) PAYE of £14,511 was deducted from Mr K's salary for 2004/05. Show the tax payable under self assessment, assuming no payments on account had been paid, and state when payment is due.   (5 marks)

(Total marks available: 40)

47   JIM SMITH

Jim Smith, aged 35, is an employee of a manufacturing company and earns a salary of £35,000 pa. He is a member of his company's contracted out pension scheme and contributes 5% of his salary. His only other benefit is the use of a company car for business and private purposes with a list price of £11,110 which was purchased last year. The CO_2 emission rate of the car is 223g/km. This benefit is not pensionable. No private petrol is provided.

His wife Sandra, aged 34, has a part-time job as a receptionist and earns £6,000 per annum.

They have £20,000 in a joint building society account which pays 3.5% net per annum. Jim has also inherited £10,000 worth of shares from his father and receives a dividend of £360 pa from the portfolio. He also receives an annual dividend of £250 from a Gilt & Fixed Interest Unit Trust.

Jim is adventurous and invested £10,000 in Enterprise Investment Scheme shares in the tax year 2004/05.

Questions:

(a) Prepare a statement of Jim's taxable income, income tax liability and income after tax and pension contributions for 2004/05. (Calculations should be rounded to the nearest £1)   (19 marks)

(b) Calculate Jim's National Insurance contributions for 2004/05 assuming he is paid monthly. Assume the monthly earnings threshold is £395.   (8 marks)

(c) What simple actions can Jim take to reduce his income tax?   (4 marks)

(d) Jim is anxious to avoid building up capital gains tax in his investment portfolio. How can he manage this problem without changing the investments he has in his portfolio?   (9 marks)

(Total marks available: 40)

48   ANDY

Andy died on 25 September 2004, leaving a widow Gill and 2 infant children. His estate at death comprised the following.

Freehold house valued at £212,500. Personal chattels at £39,500.

Quoted investments:

> 25,000 shares in COSA plc quoted at 30-34
> 10,000 shares in GA plc quoted at 111-121 with recorded bargains at 112 and 113
> 6,000 shares in ADA plc quoted at 235-240 with recorded bargains at 236 and 238

£18,000 15% loan stock valued at 67-71.

£15,000 8% loan stock valued at 92 (ex interest). Interest is paid half-yearly.

Cash in bank of £53,797.

1,000 units in the Ripoff unit trust. The published prices for each unit at death were 77 (offer) 73 (bid).

A life insurance policy payable on his death. The company paid £9,000 to his executors.

Andy owns 4,000 shares in Buzzard Ltd, an unquoted investment company with an issued share capital of 10,000 shares. Gill owns 2,000 shares. Five years ago Andy gave 1,500 shares to a registered charity who have retained the shares. The following values have been agreed:

		£
75% holding	-	100,000
60% holding	-	50,000
40% holding	-	30,000

Funeral expenses amounted to £816. In his will Andy directed that a mausoleum be built around his grave with frescos showing moments from his life. The executors paid £50,000 for this to be done.

His estate was left in trust for his children as Gill had sufficient property in her own right.

Andy was also the life tenant of two trust funds.

- The first was set up by his mother. He was the sole life tenant. The assets at death were valued at £40,000 including accrued gross interest of £400.

- The second was set up by his father. Andy and his brother David were joint life tenants, sharing income equally. The assets at death were valued at £25,000.

- David was also life tenant of a trust fund set up by an uncle. On David's death Andy would be entitled absolutely to the fund. Its assets are estimated to be worth £70,000.

Questions:

(a) Calculate the chargeable value of Andy's estate on death.   (28 marks)

(b) Calculate the IHT payable on Andy's death. He made a gift to his sister of £74,000 on the occasion of her marriage in August 2003. He has not made any other gifts.

(9 marks)

(c) Show the tax payable by the trustees and the personal representatives.   (3 marks)

(Total marks available: 40)

49   HAWKSBILL

Hawksbill died on Sunday 9 June 2004. His estate consisted of the following.

Investments:

> 20,000 shares in X plc quoted at 165p - 170p on 7 June with bargains marked at 164p, 169p and 171p, and quoted at 166p - 172p on 10 June with bargains marked at 164p, 166p, and 172p.

> 6,000 shares in Y plc quoted at 79p - 84p on 7 June and 80p - 84p on 10 June. The shares were quoted ex-div and a dividend of 5p per share was paid on 5 July 2004.

Property:

> A freehold house in London valued at £300,000 and subject to a mortgage of £85,000.

> A villa in Spain valued at £59,850.

Family company:

> Hawksbill had been managing director of his family trading company for 10 years prior to his death. The shares in the company were held as follows:

	No
Hawksbill	4,000
Wife	1,000
Son	3,000
Daughter	1,500
Trust in which Hawksbill's wife had an interest in possession	500
	10,000

The shareholdings have been unchanged since 1985. Share values at the date of death have been agreed as follows:

	£
100% holding	180,000
80%	140,000
60%	95,000
55%	80,000
40%	45,000
20%	22,000
10%	8,000

The company held a piece of land worth £30,000 as an investment.

Hawksbill also had bank balances of £16,400 including accrued interest (net) of £200.

Hawksbill had interests in two trusts as follows:

He was the life tenant of a trust in which his interest had commenced on the death of an uncle in November 2002, when the value of the trust fund was £29,200; IHT of £2,960 was paid out of the trust fund as a result of the uncle's death. On 10 June 2004, the trust fund was valued at £58,300.

He had a reversionary interest under the will of his late aunt subject to the prior life interest of his brother who was still living at 10 June 2004. The value of Hawksbill's interest at 10 June 2004 was £18,240.

At the date of his death Hawksbill had household debts of £1,340, an outstanding 2003/04 CGT liability of £3,920 and the funeral expenses amounted to £3,870 including £510 for a tombstone.

The only lifetime gift Hawksbill had ever made was in July 2000 when he set up a discretionary trust for his nephews and nieces. He transferred £255,600 to the trust and agreed to pay the IHT liability arising. The nil band at the time was £234,000.

Under the terms of his will, Hawksbill left his entire estate to his nephews and nieces.

Questions:

(a) Calculate the IHT arising on Hawksbill's lifetime gift.   (8 marks)

(b) Calculate the IHT arising on the death estate.   (32 marks)

(Total marks available: 40)

50   KEN SING

Ken Sing, aged 59, has been living in the UK since July 1996, working for the London branch of the Pajan National Bank. Ken was born in the country of Pajan, where he is domiciled, and he plans to return there when he retires in June 2005. You should assume that today's date is 5 April 2005.

Ken is paid a salary of £75,265 pa by the Pajan National Bank, and is provided with an 1,800cc motor car which cost £38,000 in 2000. The CO_2 emission level of the car is 222g/km. All running costs, including petrol, are paid for by the bank. The Pajan National Bank also pays for Ken's private medical insurance premiums of £1,200 pa, and for his £1,500 pa membership of a golf club which is used to meet clients of the bank. Ken has an interest free loan of £90,000 from the bank, which was used to purchase his private residence in London. This cost £115,000 in July 1996, and is currently worth £178,000. PAYE of £34,273 was deducted from Ken's salary during 2004/05.

Ken also owned the following assets as at 5 April 2005.

(a) A house situated in Pajan worth £120,000, which is rented out for £10,000 pa. Pajanese tax at the rate of 30% is payable on the rental income. Ken remits £3,500 of the income to the UK each year, and invests the remainder in Pajan. In December 2004 Ken sold a plot of land attached to the house for £40,000. All of the proceeds from the disposal were remitted to the UK. The house and land were purchased in March 1985 for £50,000. The house has never been Ken's principal private residence. The indexed rise to April 1998 was 0.752.

(b) 100,000 £1 ordinary shares in High-Growth plc, an investment trust quoted on the UK Stock Exchange at 102 - 110. High-Growth plc has an issued share capital of 10,000,000 shares, and paid a dividend of nine pence per share during 2004/05. Ken inherited the shares as a specific gift on the death of an uncle in September 2001 when they were worth £45,000. IHT of £13,333 was paid out of the residue of the estate on the gifts.

(c) 20,000 £1 ordinary shares in Small-Time Ltd, an unquoted UK resident trading company with an issued share capital of 80,000 shares. Ken has sat on the board of the company as a non-executive director since June 1997. This post is unpaid, and Small-Time has not paid a dividend in recent years. Ken's shareholding is worth £65,000, and was subscribed for at par in December 1993. Indexation to April 1998 is £2,918. Small-Time Ltd has assets worth £262,500 of which £12,500 are investments in quoted shares.

(d) Bank deposits of £96,000 with the Pajan National Bank, of which £76,000 is held at the London branch and £20,000 at the main branch in Pajan. Interest has been credited to these accounts in 2004/05 as follows: London branch £2,240; Pajan branch £850.

Interest is stated net of tax, which in the case of the Pajanese branch is at the rate of 15%. All of the interest arising in respect of the Pajanese branch has been remitted to the UK.

In December 2004 Ken sold a set of paintings situated in his Pajan residence for £8,000. The paintings were purchased in March 1985 for £2,800 and had an indexed cost of £4,906 at April 1998. Ken deposited the proceeds from the disposal in his bank account in Pajan.

Under the Pajanese tax system, capital gains are not subject to taxation. There is no double taxation treaty between the United Kingdom and Pajan.

Ken has been a widower for a number of years, and has left all of his assets to his children under the terms of his will.

Assume that the official rate of interest is 5%.

Questions:

(a) Calculate Ken's income tax and CGT payable for 2004/05 under self-assessment.

(20 marks)

(b) Advise Ken of his liability to IHT were he to die before returning to Pajan in June 2005. You answer should include an explanation of why Ken's assets are or are not subject to IHT, and should assume that he has no outstanding tax liabilities.

(10 marks)

QSR rates:

Period between charges	%
Less than 1 year	100
1-2 years	80
2-3 years	60
3-4 years	40
4-5 years	20

(c) When he return to Pajan, Ken plans to dispose of all of his assets situated in the UK. Advise him of his liability to CGT if he were to dispose of these assets (i) before returning to Pajan, and (ii) after returning to Pajan. You should assume that the shares in High-Growth plc will be sold for £1.02 per share, all disposals are made in June 2005, and that Ken will be liable to CGT at the rate of 40% during 2005/06.   (10 marks)

You should use the tax rates and allowances for 2004/05 throughout, and should assume that the value of Ken's assets will not materially alter in the foreseeable future.

(Total marks available: 40)

51   SEBASTIAN WORTH

Sebastian Worth died on 1 July 2004. He had made the following lifetime gifts.

(i) 7 August 1995, a gross chargeable transfer for inheritance tax of £264,000, to a discretionary trust for his son Dominic. The trustees paid the IHT arising.

(ii) 6 October 1996, a gross chargeable transfer for IHT of £69,000 to a discretionary trust for his daughter Emma, all IHT having been accounted for by the trustees.

Assume for (i) and (ii) that these amounts are net of the annual exemption.

(iii) 7 December 1998, £250 to each of 4 nephews and £83,000 to a close friend, the donees to bear any inheritance tax liability in each case.

(iv) 3 February 2001, £58,000 cash to a discretionary trust set up by Sebastian for his nieces and nephews, Sebastian to pay any inheritance tax liability arising.

(v) 13 March 2004, Sebastian gave his plant hire business, which he had owned for the past 6 years to his son Dominic. The business consisted of the following assets which were transferred as follows. The premises, valued at £42,300; the plant hire equipment, valued at £24,200; and the stock of machine spares, valued at £1,700.

On his death, Sebastian left chargeable assets valued at £274,000 and his general debts and funeral expenses came to £3,780.

During his lifetime, Sebastian had given an unlimited guarantee to a bank in respect of an overdraft granted to his brother, Bob. In March 2004 Bob filed his own petition in bankruptcy which showed he had no assets of any value. The bank indicated to Worth's executors that it would claim against his estate for the full amount of the overdraft (including interest) of £6,000.

At the date of Sebastian's death, the business premises given to his son Dominic were worth only £36,000 and the plant hire equipment £23,200. The business was however still being run at the date of Sebastian's death by Dominic.

By his will, Sebastian left £60,000 to his wife and the residue of his estate to his daughter Emma.

Included in Sebastian's estate is business property worth £120,000 (not included in the figure of £274,000 above). This represented his unincorporated photography business. The business was left to his wife together with the £60,000 and she intends to sell it as soon as possible as she knows nothing about photography.

Dominic and Emma feel that their father has not distributed his estate in the most tax efficient way.

Questions:

(a) Calculate the inheritance tax liabilities arising as a result of the gifts made in December 1998, February 2001, March 2004 and death in July 2004, stating in the case of the liabilities arising on death who is liable for their payment.   (24 marks)

(b) Advise Dominic and Emma as to the feasibility of adjusting their father's dispositions, the conditions that must be satisfied together with proposals for a more tax efficient method.   (8 marks)

Dominic wrote to you on 3 May 2004 on various matters, including the following in relation to capital gains tax:

'I recently read an article in the financial columns of a newspaper which explained the meaning of residence, ordinary residence and domicile. Unfortunately, that article did not consider the relevance of these concepts in determining taxation liabilities. I am particularly concerned with the capital gains tax implications and I should be grateful if you would explain the significance of those terms in relation to that tax.'

(c) Explain the relevance of residence, ordinary residence and domicile in determining an individual's liability to capital gains.   (8 marks)

(Total marks available: 40)

52   LEN SHACKLETON

Len Shackleton, made the following lifetime transfers

1 October 2004   £275,000 to his friend Charlie Hurley
2 May 2007   £270,000 to a discretionary trust, the trust paying any tax arising

He died on 2 June 2009 leaving his considerable estate of £600,000 split equally between Raich Carter and Billy Hughes.

Len had made no other gifts beforehand nor did he make any subsequently.

Ignore annual exemptions and assume the tax rates/exemptions do not change.

Questions:

(a) Calculate the IHT arising at the point these gifts were made, and any further tax that would arise on death.   (20 marks)

(b) Raich is married to the chairman of the board of a privatised water company and does not need his inheritance. He would rather his children received the benefit.

     (i)   What is the most tax efficient way of doing this?   (2 marks)
     (ii)   How does this method work?   (5 marks)
     (iii)   What conditions need to be satisfied in order that this plan can be carried out?

                                                    (7 marks)

(c) Policies could have been taken out to mitigate the effects of Inheritance Tax. With the benefit of hindsight, describe what kind of policies could have been used, what type of trust should have been used and the beneficiaries of the trust in each of the following cases:

     (i)   with regard to the gift made in 2004   (3 marks)
     (ii)   with regard to the net estate on death   (3 marks)

                                       (Total marks available: 40)

53   TANNIA WHITING

Tannia Whiting is a single parent born 7 July 1961. She has a son, Adam, born 1 April 1988.

Tannia started in business as a freelance garden designer on 6 April 2002 and makes up accounts to 5 April each year. Her taxable profits have been:

2002/03 £35,000
2003/04 £40,000
2004/05 £40,500

Tannia started a stakeholder pension in April 2004 and made regular contributions of £200 (net) per month.

In 2004/05 Tannia also received interest of £240 from a local authority bond and a dividend of £2,700 from a unit trust. In previous years she had no other income other than her business earnings.

Adam was recently left a legacy of £2,500 under the will of his grandmother. He has a spare-time job which pays him £7,000 pa. He intends to go away to college to study next year and may need the legacy to pay tuition fees.

Assume the date is now 1 May 2005.

Questions:

(a) Calculate, **showing all your workings,** the amount of income tax payable or repayable by Tannia for tax year 2004/05, taking into account the payments on account that Tannia was required to make. Ignore national insurance contributions and tax credits.

(25 marks)

(b) Calculate the amount of any additional contribution that Tannia can make to her stakeholder pension for 2004/05, state the conditions for carrying back the contribution to that year and comment on the effect of such an election being made. **You are not required to calculate the tax repayment arising.** (10 marks)

(c) State your recommendation for investment in relation to the legacy left to Adam by his grandmother. (5 marks)

(Total marks available: 40)

54   SALLY AND GEORGE

Sally will be aged 70 on 12 December 2004. She is married to George who is aged 63.

Both are retired.

They have provided you with the following details of their income for the tax year 2004/05.

	Sally £	George £
State Pension (gross)	1,060	
Private pension (gross)	8,350	17,400
Building society interest (net)	1,100	300
Dividends (net)	750	580
Corporate Bond PEP income received	200	

In addition you have identified that George has accumulation units in the ABC unit trust. He has given you the following details for 2004/05:

Income reinvested £600, equalisation within this figure £40.

Sally has recently switched funds within a Luxembourg offshore SICAV umbrella fund. The fund does not have distributor status. The switch realised £15,000 for reinvestment within the SICAV. The cost of the original investment was £13,500. Sally is very diligent and also provides you with an indexation figure relating to this investment of 0.225.

Questions:

(a) Calculate George's income tax liability for 2004/05. (20 marks)

(b) Calculate Sally's income tax liability for 2004/05. (15 marks)

(c) Calculate the income tax saved if George were to transfer all of his investments to Sally. (5 marks)

(Total marks available: 40)

55   ROY AND CYBILLE

Roy is 70 years old and married to Cybille who is aged 67. Both are at the moment in good health. Roy's estate is valued at £400,000 and Cybille's at £340,000. They have two children aged 37 and 35, who already have substantial assets of their own, each of whom have two minor children. Neither Roy nor Cybille have made, or intend to make, any substantial lifetime gifts.

Roy and Cybille have made wills which leave everything to each other. If the other spouse has already died, that spouse's estate passes to the children in equal shares. Roy and Cybille understand that the spouse exemption will apply on the first death of them, but are concerned about inheritance tax on the second death.

They have heard that it is a good idea to make sure that nil rate band for inheritance tax is used on the first death by establishing a nil rate band discretionary trust. The family have decided that neither of the adult children should be beneficiaries of the trust, but that the grandchildren should be beneficiaries.

Questions:

(a) (i) Explain how a nil rate band discretionary trust in a will works and the IHT charges that may arise on it. (8 marks)

    (ii) Set out why it is a good idea to use such a trust. (6 marks)

    (iii) How could the surviving spouse be reassured that he/she will benefit from the nil rate band discretionary trust if the need arose? (4 marks)

(b) Explain the powers of investment that trustees would have under the Trustee Act 2000. (10 marks)

(c) How would the rule against accumulations affect the discretionary trust? (7 marks)

(d) A few years later, the wills have been redrafted to include a nil rate band discretionary trust. Roy dies. After six months one of the trustees, a local solicitor, also dies. There are then two remaining trustees. The trustees and the family agree that it would be a good idea to appoint a replacement trustee. Who can appoint the new trustee and how must it be done? (5 marks)

(Total marks available: 40)

56 BILL WATTS

Bill Watts died recently. In his will he had established a trust to provide income for his wife Mary during her lifetime, the capital to pass to their only son Dick, aged 16, on her death. A significant proportion of the assets held in this trust is made up of a patent for an invention. This patent brings in a good income but it expires in the year 2016.

Mary has expressed concern about the funding of Dick's further education and is considering setting up an Accumulation and Maintenance trust for his benefit.

Questions:

(a) The trustees of Bill Watts trust for Dick understand that the patent is a 'wasting asset'. If Bill Watts made no specific instructions in his will regarding the patent, what are the trustees' duties in this case regarding the Life Tennant and the Remainderman? (14 marks)

(b) One of the trustees of Bill Watt's trust is an old drinking partner of his. Mary would prefer not to deal with him and asks her solicitor if there are any circumstances under which he can be replaced as a trustee. What would be her solicitor's advice? (6 marks)

(c) (i) If the trustees of Mary's proposed A&M trust distribute income to Dick, what are the income tax implications? (4 marks)

    (ii) Explain the Capital Gains Tax position of an A&M trust both within the trust and on the distribution of cash from the sale of assets held in the trust. (4 marks)

(iii) What would be the Inheritance Tax implications of Mary's gift to the trust?

(5 marks)

(iv) How would this trust differ from other forms of discretionary trusts in terms of IHT?

(7 marks)

(Total marks available: 40)

57   **DONALD MANTON**

You recently met Donald Manton, aged 63. He is a keen investor in number of different areas and he has given you the following details of his investments.

General investments

Donald is retired and has a pension of £22,600 gross for the current tax year.

Investment income from gilts of £5,000 gross

Maxi ISA from which he hopes to receive £350 income this tax year

In addition he has the following National Savings products:

	Rate	
Series 18 Pensioner Guaranteed Income Bonds	4.75%	£15,000 invested 3/2/02
57rd issue Fixed Interest Savings Certificates	3.55%	£100,000 invested 13/3/02
Ordinary account	1.35%	£20,000 invested 20/12/99

Property investments

Donald also owns a number of properties, both freehold and leasehold. Details are as follows.

(a) A holiday cottage near Seahouses, Northumberland. He received gross annual rents of £11,000. The property has been owned by Donald for eight years. He paid the following expenses:

	£
Ground rent	75
Letting agency fees	1,100
Accountancy fees	500
Insurance cover for lost rentals	100

(b) In April 2004, Donald granted a short lease on a retail shop to a former work colleague, who paid Donald a premium of £17,000. The lease is for 20 years and the annual rent is £2,000.

(c) Donald also lets out a room in his main residence for which he receives a yearly rental of £6,200 on which he incurs expenses of £800. He also claims the relevant relief available to him.

Capital gains

In the tax year 2004/05, he disposed of the following assets:

(a) All his equity unit trust units of which 10,000 were purchased in August 1987 for £26,500 (indexed pool cost £37,814 at April 1998). He invested a further £5,500 in 2,400 units in February 2002. The unit trust units were sold in September 2004 for £31,000.

(b) A plot of land was partly disposed of in August 2004 for £20,000. The value of the remaining land was £15,000. It was originally purchased in November 1984 for £12,000. The land was not used for business purposes. Indexed rise to April 1998 was 0.787.

(c) Donald acquired an unquoted shareholding on 1 December 1980 for £20,000. The value of the holding at 31.3.82 was £25,000. Donald sold the shareholding for £150,000 on 1 December 2004. The company was a trading company and the shareholding represented 30% of the ordinary shares in the company. Indexed rise to April 1998 was 1.047 from March 1982.

You should use the above information to answer the following questions, **showing all your workings** where appropriate.

Questions:

(a) Calculate, for each property, the amount of **rental income** assessable for Income Tax purposes. (15 marks)

(b) Calculate the amount of gross taxable income Donald will receive from his earned income and investment income (other than the rental income) for the 2004/05 tax year.

(8 marks)

(c) With regard to the capital gains, using the retail price indices shown above:

    (i)   Calculate the gain and/or loss arising on the **equity unit trust units**. (8 marks)

    (ii)   Calculate the indexed gain or loss arising on the **land**. (6 marks)

    (iii)   Calculate the indexed gain or loss on the unquoted shareholding. (9 marks)

    (iv)   Using the taper relief percentages shown in the Tax Tables, show the taxable gains for Donald in 2004/05. (9 marks)

(d) Calculate the income tax and capital gains tax payable by Donald in 2004/2005.

(7 marks)

(e) Outline to Donald the conditions that would need to be fulfilled for the holiday cottage to be treated as a furnished holiday letting. (7 marks)

(f) Donald is considering disposing of the holiday cottage during 2004/05. The disposal would be to a third party. He is undecided what to do with the proceeds but would like your advice concerning the reliefs that could be available to him to mitigate or reduce his CGT liability. Assume that the cottage qualifies as a furnished holiday letting.

Identify the conditions that must be met by Donald in order to qualify for rollover relief.

(6 marks)

(Total marks available: 75)

58   TOM JONES

Tom Jones is a widower, aged 58 and is in good health. His wife died in August 2004.

Tom has taken voluntary redundancy and early retirement with effect from 5 November 2004. He received an ex gratia redundancy package of £60,000 and a lump sum of £30,000 of cash from his company final salary contracted in scheme.

His salary was £42,000 and he now receives an index linked pension of £16,000 pa. Tom's gross taxable investment income is £6,000 (from building society accounts).

Tom was a member of an unapproved share option scheme. In December 2001 he was granted the option to acquire 4,000 shares in his employer's company. The exercise price was £2.60. He exercised his option in June 2004 when the prevailing market price of the shares was £4.10. He subsequently sold the shares in September 2004 for £4.00.

Tom has accumulated savings and received a significant inheritance some years ago. His estate is estimated to be worth £400,000 excluding the redundancy pay and the cash lump sum. His will leaves his estate to his two daughters in equal shares.

Tom has decided to gift his severance cash to his grandchildren. His eldest daughter has two children aged 13 and 10; his youngest daughter is aged 22 and has only recently married. He wishes the gift to be held in trust with the income reinvested until the children are 21 at which age they should have the right to the capital. Tom has made no earlier gifts.

Questions:

(a) (i)   Prepare a statement showing his income tax liability for the year ending April 2005. (14 marks)

    (ii)   Calculate his National Insurance liability for 2004/05. The monthly earnings threshold is £395. (4 marks)

(b) Give reasons as to why a Bare Trust would *not* be suitable for the proposed gift to his grandchildren. (3 marks)

(c) (i)   What are the potential inheritance tax implications if the gift was made by means of transfer into an Accumulation and Maintenance Trust? (6 marks)

    (ii)   What type of life assurance would be most appropriate for any IHT liability arising as a result of this gift? Give details of the sum assured, the grantee and the life assured. (4 marks)

    (iii) Advise on the most appropriate trust for the life assurance policy and outline who should be the trustee(s) and beneficiaries of the life assurance policy. (8 marks)

(d) Tom has decided to use an Accumulation and Maintenance Trust for the gift itself.

    (i)   Outline the constraints on the beneficial interests of the trust. (5 marks)

    (ii)   Outline the taxation of income and capital gains as a result of the gift and its transfer into the trust. (9 marks)

    (iii) Outline the IHT treatment of the beneficiaries' interests in the trust. (3 marks)

(e) (i)   Advise Tom as to who should be the trustee(s) of this Accumulation and Maintenance Trust. (6 marks)

    (ii)   What procedures should be adopted if one of the trustees were to die? (4 marks)

    (iii) Under what circumstances will the trustees be able to charge for their time in the administration of the trust? (3 marks)

(f) Comment briefly on the suitability of the following types of assets as underlying investments for the Accumulation and Maintenance Trust.

    (i)   ISA (2 marks)
    (ii)   High yielding corporate bonds (2 marks)
    (iii) Index linked gilts (2 marks)

(Total marks available: 75)

59   DAVID STAMP

Personal Details

David Stamp, aged 50, lives in London. He has two children; Martha aged 16 and John aged 14 by his first marriage. His children live with their mother.

Two years ago David married Concepta, aged 32, who works as a Spanish Bullfighter.

Residence

David is UK resident and is domiciled in the UK. He manages to spend 2 months each year in his villa in Spain. Concepta, who is ordinarily resident and domiciled in Spain, rarely manages to spend more than one month in the UK each year.

Business

David sold his business on 6th August 2004. He had started the business from scratch in 1983. The purchaser paid £100,000 for the goodwill. The only other chargeable asset was a freehold shop. David had acquired the shop in August 1985 for £30,000. He added an extension costing £25,000 in November 2002. The purchaser paid £150,000 for the shop.

Indexation allowance August 1985 – April 1998 = 0.703.

Investments

David purchased a managed bond from Listless Life on 1st August 1999 when he invested £50,000. The current value is £75,000.

Income

David expects a total gross income (after personal allowance) of £27,500 from all sources for the tax year 2004/05.

Gifts

David is intending to give £80,000 to Concepta so that she can repay some debts and put her younger brother through university.

David has also decided to give £1,000 pa to a registered charity.

Trust

David set up a discretionary trust for the benefit of his children two years ago. In the tax year 2004/05 the accounts show the following:

Dividends from shares	£6,000
Building society interest	£3,200
Administrative expenses	£800

Inheritance

Great Aunt Matilda left £50,000 to David's father when she died 10 months ago. David's father left this inheritance specifically in his will to Martha. Unfortunately he died 4 months later.

Power of attorney

David's Uncle Albert is in failing health for the past few years. He has asked if David can look after his affairs in the future if he becomes mentally incapable of doing this himself.

Questions:

(a)   (i)   Calculate the capital gain tax payable by David on the sale of his business.

(11 marks)

(ii) David has decided to invest in furnished holiday accommodation. How can that help his capital gains tax position? (4 marks)

(b) (i) David is thinking about cashing in his managed bond. Calculate the likely income tax payable on disposal if he does so. Assume the date is 5 April 2005. (12 marks)

(ii) If David made a partial encashment of, say, £40,000 how would that be treated by the Inland Revenue? (2 marks)

(iii) Explain the importance of segmentation with regard to partial encashment. (3 marks)

(c) Calculate the total income tax payable by the trustees of David's discretionary trust for the tax year 2004/05. (7 marks)

(d) (i) Explain the inheritance tax treatment of Great Aunt Matilda's legacy to David's father when it passes on to Martha. (5 marks)

(ii) What are the inheritance tax consequences of David's gift to Concepta? (5 marks)

(iii) David intends to retire soon to Spain and become non resident for UK tax purposes. What effect would this have on his inheritance tax planning in view of the fact that he does not wish his estate to be subject to UK inheritance tax? (5 marks)

(e) State the type of arrangement which is required to enable David to act for Uncle Albert in the future and explain how this arrangement will work in practice. (4 marks)

(f) David has heard about Individual Savings Accounts and would like to know more. Outline briefly the main types of investment that can be included in an ISA. (9 marks)

(g) (i) Briefly explain how David's gifts to charity may be made in a tax efficient way. (3 marks)

(ii) If David decided to give a lump sum of £5,000 instead of regular gifts how would the gift be treated in terms of income tax and inheritance tax. (5 marks)

(Total marks available: 75)

60   KEITH AND ANN

Keith and Ann are aged 35 and 36 respectively. Keith is a higher rate taxpayer. Ann has decided to stay at home to look after the two children; she has no earned income and is a non-taxpayer.

They have two children Emma aged 7 and Tim aged 5.

Their assets are as follows:

	£ Keith	£ Ann	£ Joint
Cash (see below)	35,000		
Investments	80,000	98,000	
Personal effects	15,000	17,000	
Family home - owned as tenants in common			200,000

In addition Keith has Death in Service cover through his work. He has completed a nomination form in favour of his wife. The cover is currently worth £120,000.

He also has an endowment policy on his own life. The policy is not assigned nor is it in a trust since he sees it primarily as a savings vehicle. The sum assured is £65,000.

Ann's parents are aged 71, and are both in good health. They are both basic rate taxpayers.

They have estimated their net worth to be £355,000. Her father's estate is worth £185,000 and her mother's estate is worth £170,000. Their wills currently leave their respective estates to each other, and if they are the last surviving spouse then their estate passes to Ann as their only child.

Keith has recently received £35,000 as a win on the premium bonds. It is currently held in a cash deposit account.

He wishes to gift this to his children with a view to them having a capital sum available to them when they are in their early 20s to ease the strain of becoming financially independent.

Keith is considering using a trust as a means of investing the gift to his children.

Questions:

(a) If he were to use bare trusts, what would be the tax implications on both him and his children? Organise your answer under the following headings.

   (i)   Income tax   (3 marks)
   (ii)   Capital gains tax   (4 marks)
   (iii) Inheritance Tax   (3 marks)

(b) He is also considering using an accumulation and maintenance trust for this gift.

   (i)   Outline the essential requirements of such a trust for Keith.   (6 marks)

   (ii)   Explain the potential CGT liabilities during the life of such a trust assuming that income and capital vest at the same time.   (5 marks)

   (iii) How might section 31 of the Trustee Act 1925 affect the CGT position and how this could be avoided.   (7 marks)

(c) Assume that Keith proceeds with an accumulation and maintenance trust for the gift to his children. You have short listed either a UK based single premium insurance bond or investment trust zero coupon preference shares as the underlying investment.

   (i)   Explain the actual and potential charges to tax on both the bond itself and its taxation within the trust. Detail how such liability can be minimised.

                                                                                                     (12 marks)

   (ii)   Explain how the zero coupon investment trust shares are taxed and detail what steps can be taken to reduce the actual tax payable while they are held within the trust.   (7 marks)

(d) You have discovered that Keith and Ann have not made wills. Explain, with workings, how Keith's estate would be allocated if he were to predecease Ann. Assume that Keith has gifted the £35,000 win to his children.   (10 marks)

(e) Calculate the inheritance tax saving if Ann's parents were to include a survivorship clause in their wills. Assume that both deaths occurred within 2 months of November 2004.   (4 marks)

(f) Ann's parents are considering discretionary wills.

   (i)   Describe the basic principles and requirements of a discretionary will.

                                                                                                     (10 marks)

   (ii)   Explain the potential advantages of such an arrangement.   (4 marks)

(Total marks available: 75 marks)

61   JOE POLLARD

Your client is Joe Pollard, whom you met recently. Assume that the meeting took place on 10 April 2004. He gave you the following information:

Personal details

Aged 49
Divorced, one daughter, Laura aged 27

Business

Self employed dentist in private practice. Acquired practice on 1 May 2002 for £300,000.

Purchase price includes freehold surgery, goodwill and other assets.

Funded purchase price with loan of £200,000 (secured on the freehold) and savings of £100,000.

The current value of the practice, including the freehold, is £375,000.

Prior to 1 May 2002 was employed in another dental practice.

Divorce

Separated from wife, Ruth, on 13 March 1999. Joe made a voluntary lump sum payment to Ruth on 13 December 1999 of £50,000. Decree absolute was granted on 17 June 2000. Under a court order, Joe was ordered to pay a further lump sum of £20,000 and he did this on 23 February 2002. No maintenance payments were ordered.

House

Joe owns the house in which he lives. There is no mortgage and the current value is £170,000.

Lifetime gifts

Joe and Laura are keen scuba divers. On her 18th birthday in 1994, Joe gave Laura his cottage in Cornwall, which he had used as a base for diving trips. It was agreed that if Joe ever wanted to use the cottage, he would be able to do so free of charge. Joe has taken two weeks holiday at Easter and four weeks holiday in August in the cottage every year since 1995. The value of the cottage in 1994 was £30,000. It is now worth £45,000.

Quoted shares

Fantastic Flippers plc, 150,000 ordinary 10p shares quoted at 50.25 ex div.

The shares were bought by Joe on 23 October 2003 and cost £35,000.

The company declared a dividend of 8p per share, payable to shareholders on its register at 25 March 2004. The dividend is due for payment on 2 May 2004.

Other assets

Midcounties Building Society investment account £20,000.

Liabilities

Income tax £45,000.

Bank loan as above.

Unsecured loan of £25,000 from Joe's mother and used to pay part of the lump sums to Ruth.

Pension scheme

Joe started a personal pension scheme policy in 1988. His fund is currently worth £85,000. In the event of his death before retirement, the policy will pay out the then current fund value.

Under the scheme rules, Joe has power to nominate a benefit to anyone he wishes. To date he has not exercised that power.

Will

Joe's will provides for his estate to pass to Laura.

Father's will trust

Joe and his brother, Ben, are beneficiaries of their father's discretionary will trust. Joe has been told by the trustees that the estimated income and tax payable by the trustees for the year ended 5 April 2005 is likely to be:

Dividends (net)	£15,750
Building society interest (net)	£3,600
Accountancy fees attributable to income	£450
Further income tax payable by the trustees	£4,725

Questions:

(a) Joe is concerned about the inheritance tax payable on his estate. Explain how the following items will be treated in computing the value of Joe's estate for IHT purposes, assuming that Joe dies during 2004. Give brief reasons for your answers.

    (i)   The first lump sum to Ruth   **(4 marks)**

    (ii)   The second lump sum to Ruth   **(3 marks)**

    (iii) The cottage in Cornwall   **(4 marks)**

    (iv) The dental practice (you should consider the position if Joe dies in April 2004 and alternatively if he dies in June 2004)   **(6 marks)**

(b) If Joe had died on 12 April 2004, prepare calculations to show:

    (i)   the value of Joe's estate for inheritance tax purposes.   **(15 marks)**

    (ii)   the amount of IHT payable on that estate.   **(5 marks)**

(c) Joe is anxious to reduce the amount of IHT payable on his death. Describe what he could do to achieve this and calculate the amount of tax saved in respect of:

    (i)   the personal pension scheme   **(5 marks)**

    (ii)   the cottage in Cornwall   **(6 marks)**

(d) Joe is surprised that his father's trust should have additional income tax to pay, in addition to tax suffered at source.

    (i)   Explain why the trust has further income tax to pay.   **(4 marks)**

    (ii)   Prepare workings to show how the further charge to tax of £4,725 is calculated.

                                                                    (12 marks)

(e) Joe would like to make provision for good causes in his will, by establishing a charitable trust. State three tax advantages arising in respect of a charitable trust, as opposed to a non-charitable trust.   **(6 marks)**

(f) Describe to Joe how a further investment into Fantastic Flippers could be sheltered from income tax and capital gains tax.   **(5 marks)**

(Total marks available: 75)

Answer
bank

1 **HARRY**

	Non-savings income £	Savings income £	Dividends £	
	30,000			
$1,800 \times \dfrac{100}{80}$		2,250		*1 mark*
$4,000 \times \dfrac{100}{90}$			4,444	*1 mark*
Personal allowance	(4,745)	-		
Taxable income	25,255	2,250	4,444	*1 mark*

On non-savings income

2,020 @ 10%	202	*1 mark*
23,235 @ 22%	5,111	*1 mark*
25,255		

* unused basic rate band = 31,400 – 25,255 = 6,145

On savings income
* all in basic rate band 2,250 @ 20% → 450 *1 mark*
* remaining basic rate band 6,145 – 2,250 = 3,895

On Dividends

3,895 @ 10%	389	*1 mark*
549 @ 32.5%	178	*1 mark*
4,444		
Income tax liability	6,330	

Tutor's comments

Remember to separate out the income into the three categories. The personal allowance is set against non-savings income first. This gives the least tax.

2 **TAX CREDIT**

Maximum tax credit

		£	
CTC	- family element	545	*1 mark*
	- child element	1,625	*1 mark*
WTC	- basic element	1,570	*1 mark*
	- one parent element	1,545	*1 mark*
	- 30 hour element	640	*1 mark*
		5,925	
Earnings		16,000	
Less threshold		(5,060)	
Excess income		10,940	*1 mark*
Maximum tax credit		5,925	
Less 37% of excess income		(4,048)	*1 mark*
Award		1,877	*1 mark*

BPP
PROFESSIONAL EDUCATION

3   GIFT AID

		Non-savings income £
Pension/STI		45,000
PA		(4,745)
Taxable income		40,255

Tax:	2,020 @ 10%	202
29,380 + (100/78 × 5,460) =	36,380 @ 22%	8,003
	1,855 @ 40%	742
	40,255	8,947
Less: Tax already suffered – PAYE		(8,576)
IT remaining payable		371

1 mark (Pension/STI)
1 mark *1 mark* (PA / Taxable income)
1 mark *1 mark* *1 mark* (Tax lines)
1 mark (Less / IT remaining)
Total: 7 marks

4   BILL SMITH

1 mark — Gross income £19,200 exceeds age allowance of £18,900 by £300

1 mark — Age allowance £6,830 reduced by **£1 for every £2 over limit**

1 mark — Age allowance reduced by £150 to £6,680

Calculation:

	£
Income	19,200
Less adjusted age allowance	(6,680)
Taxable income	12,520
Tax	
2,020 @ 10%	202
10,500 @ 22%	2,310
Total Tax	2,512

1 mark (Less adjusted age allowance)
1 mark (Taxable income)
1 mark (2,020 @ 10%)
1 mark (10,500 @ 22%)
Total: 7 marks

5   ACCOMMODATION

	£
Annual value	3,000
+ (175,000 – 75,000) × 5%	5,000
Contribution	(2,500)
Assessable benefit	5,500

1 mark (Annual value)
1 mark (+ (175,000 – 75,000) × 5%)
1 mark (Contribution)
Total: 3 marks

6   CAR AND FUEL BENEFIT

1 mark — (a) (i) Cash equivalent: 15% × 14,000 (rounded down to 145g/km) £2,100

1 mark — (ii) 17% × 14,000 (155 – 145 = 10 ÷ 5 = 2 + 15 = 17%) £2,380

1 mark — (b) (i) £14,400 × 15% £2,160

1 mark — (ii) £14,400 × 17% £2,448

1 mark *1 mark* — (c) Since he only has the car for 6 months, his car and fuel benefit is $\frac{6}{12} \times (2,100 + 2,160)$

= 2,130

Total: 6 marks

7   **MR TYE**

   (a) Class 1 – employee   *1 mark*

$$\frac{15,000}{52} = £288.46$$

	£	
51 weeks × 11% × (288.46 – 91)	1,107.75	*1 mark*
1 week × 11% × (610 – 91)	57.09	*1 mark*
		Total: 4 marks
1 week × 1% × (7,288.46 – 610)	66.78	
	1,231.62	

In the week the bonus is received the earnings get capped @ £610 for the main rate.

   (b) Class 1 – director, so use annual limits £15,000 + £7,000= £22,000   *1 mark*

        £(22,000 – 4,745) = £17,255 × 11%   £1,898.05   *1 mark*

                                                        Total: 2 marks

8   **CLASS 2 NICS**

- Class 2 NICs are a **flat rate contribution** of £2.05 per week   *1 mark*

- Paid by the self employed unless earning £4,215 pa or less   *2 marks*

- And have applied for certificate of exemption   *1 mark*

                                                         Total: 4 marks

Tutor's comment

Most of this information could have been obtained from the Tax Tables available in the examination. Make sure you know what information the Tables contain.

9   **JOE JOSEPH**

£13,000 less annual exemption of £8,200 = £4,800 gain   *1 mark*

£4,800 **added to income** to calculate tax   *1 mark*

Basic rate band left £31,400 – 26,800 = 4,600   *1 mark*

£4,600 @ 20% =	920	*1 mark*
£200 @ 40% =	80	*1 mark*
Total Tax =	£1,000	*Total: 5 marks*

10   **LOSSES**

	£	
Gains	13,000	
Losses	(3,000)	
	10,000	*1 mark*
AE	(8,200)	*1 mark*
	1,800	
Loss brought forward	(1,800)	*1 mark*
	-	
		Total: 3 marks

Loss left to c/f (6,000 – 1,800) = 4,200

Tutor's comment

The current year losses have to be taken in full, but brought forward losses can be restricted to preserve the use of the annual exemption.

11 PATRICK

	£
Proceeds	225,000
Less: cost	(185,364)
Gain	39,636

1 mark

1 mark

The asset is a business asset for taper relief because it is used in Patrick's business as a greengrocer.

1 mark

Gain after taper relief (10 January 2003 – 9 January 2004 = 1 year)

1 mark

£39,636 × 50%   19,818

Total: 4 marks

12 CONSTANT

Post 5 April 1998 holding

	£
	7,000

1 mark Proceeds $\frac{1,000}{2,000}$ × £14,000

1 mark

Less: cost	(4,000)
Gain	3,000

FA 1985 pool

1 mark Proceeds $\frac{1,000}{2,000}$ × £14,000   7,000

1 mark

Less: cost	(5,000)
Unindexed gain	2,000

1 mark

Less; indexation allowance £(8,715 – 5,000)	
= 3,715 restricted to	(2,000)
Indexed gain	nil

1 mark

Total taper before taper relief £(3,000 + nil)   3,000

Total: 6 marks

13 MAXWELL

(a)   £

Deemed proceeds =	210,000
Cost	(75,000)
IA 1.047 × 75,000	(78,525)
	56,475

1 mark

1 mark

(i)   No GR claim:

Gain for Maxwell (6 years tapering) 25% × 56,475 = £14,118

1 mark

Base cost for son = 210,000

Total: 3 marks

(ii) GR claim made

No gain for Maxwell

1 mark

Base cost for son = 210,000 – 56,475 = 153,525

(b) (i)   No GR claim: answer as above – as parties are connected market value is used to calculate Maxwell's gain.

(ii) GR claim made

	£
Deemed gain (as above)	56,475
Excess of actual proceeds over	
Cost (95k – 75k) chargeable	(20,000)
Eligible for gift relief	36,475

Gain for Maxwell (6 years tapering) 25% × 20,000 = 5,000

Base cost for son = 210,000 – 36,475 = 173,525

1 mark
1 mark
1 mark
Total: 3 marks

Tutor's comments

Note how the taper relief is lost if a gift relief claim is made.

14 JACOB

	£
Gain arising	80,000
Proceeds reinvested	95,000

∴ *maximum* EIS reinvestment relief claim will be £80,000

Taper relief applies for non business asset (3 years, 95%)

Jacob should leave gains of (8,200 × 100/95) = £8,632 to utilise AE and taper relief, so he should claim EIS reinvestment relief of (80,000 – 8,632) = £71,638.

1 mark
1 mark
1 mark
Total: 3 marks

Tutor's comments

This is the only relief where a claim can be made to keep AE, losses and taper relief, in charge.

15 GLENDA

	Total Income £		UK income £	
Schedule E - UK	25,815		25,815	
- Foreign	12,000			
Interest income	1,525		1,525	*1 mark*
	39,340		27,340	
PA	(4,745)		(4,745)	*1 mark*
Taxable	34,595		22,595	
				1 mark
2,020 @ 10%	202	2,020 @ 10%	202	
29,380 @ 22%	6,464	19,050 @ 22%	4,191	*1 mark*
31,400		21,070★		
3,195 @ 40%	1,278	1,525 @ 20%	305	*1 mark*
34,595	7,944		4,698	
Tax on total income			7,944	*1 mark*
DTR – lower of				*1 mark*
(i) foreign tax £4,400				
(ii) UK tax on foreign source (7,944 – 4,698 = £3,246)			(3,246)	
Tax liability			4,698	*Total: 7 marks*

★ £(25,815 – 4,745) = £21,070

Tutor's comments

The foreign income is treated as the top slice of income for working out DTR. This means that DTR is the difference between the tax on total income and the tax on UK source income only.

16 RESIDENCE

1 mark
A liability to CGT may arise if the individual is carrying on a trade, profession or vocation in the UK through a branch or agency.

1 mark
This happens when an asset which has been used for the purposes of the branch or agency is disposed of.

1 mark
A charge will also arise if the UK trade, profession or vocation ceases or the asset is taken out of the UK.

1 mark
In these last two cases, there is a deemed disposal of the asset at market value.

1 mark
Individuals who have acquired assets before they leave the UK for a period of residence outside the UK for a period of less than 5 tax years remain chargeable on those assets whilst abroad.

1 mark
Gains made in the year of departure will be taxed in that year.

1 mark
Total: 7 marks
Later gains will be charged in the year of return to the UK.

Tutor's comments

You may have thought that there was a charge for non-UK residents on all assets situated in the UK. This is not the case. The general rule is that individuals who are neither UK-resident nor UK ordinarily resident are not liable to CGT. The two cases above are exceptions to this rule.

17 MR ARM

LIFE TAX

		£
1.	CLT (23/8/01)	243,000
	(No AE's as already allocated to PET earlier in same fiscal year)	-
	Life tax payable	243,000

$$(243,000 - 242,000 \star) \times \frac{20}{80} = 250$$

1 mark
Gross chargeable transfer   243,250 (243,000 + 250)

1 mark
$\star$ First chargeable transfer during life therefore none of the nil band has been used. Note that the earlier PET to the daughter is not subject to lifetime tax.

DEATH TAX

		£
1.	PET (5/01)	155,000
	AE - 01/02	(3,000)
	- 00/01 b/f	(3,000)
	Gross chargeable transfer	149,000

1 mark

1 mark
No tax payable - covered by nil band of £263,000.

2. CLT (8/01) gross chargeable transfer (above) 243,250
    40% × (243,250 – 114,000 *) 51,700 *1 mark*
    Less: life tax paid (250) *1 mark*
    IHT payable on death by trustees 51,450

    Death 2 to 3 years after gift so no taper relief
    * Nil band left
       Nil band at death 263,000
       Gross chargeable transfers
       in 7 years before gift (149,000) *1 mark*
       Nil band left 114,000

3. Estate - exempt because left to wife. *Total: 7 marks*

18 HENRY

	£
Value of shares	100,000

less BPR (exclude excepted assets) *2 marks*

$$100,000 \times \frac{(1,000 - 170)}{1,000} = 83,000 \qquad (83,000)$$

1 mark

So value in estate = 17,000

Total: 3 marks

19 MR L

	£
Chargeable estate	327,000

IHT at full rates (327 – 263) × 40% 25,600 *1 mark*
Less: QSR *2 marks*

$$8,420 \times \frac{40,111}{48,531} \times 20\% \text{ (4-5 years)} \qquad (1,392)$$

1 mark

IHT payable on estate 24,208 *Total: 4 marks*

20 TAPER RELIEF

- It applies to lifetime transfers where tax has become payable as a result of the donor dying within 7 years of making the gift *1 mark*

- The donor must have survived 3 years for any taper relief to be given *1 mark*

- It applies to PETs which become chargeable *1 mark*

- And to chargeable lifetime transfers where more tax might become payable *1 mark*

- It will benefit the recipients of the gifts *1 mark*
  Total: 5 marks

Tutor's comment

Don't mix up IHT taper relief and CGT taper relief!

21 CUTHBERT

(a) No IHT implications. Small gifts exemption *2 marks*

(b) Gift to an A&M trust is a PET *1 mark*
     No immediate tax liability *1 mark*
     No IHT after 7 years. Tapering relief up to 7 years. *2 marks*
     Total: 4 marks

(c) • Gift to discretionary trust is a chargeable lifetime transfer

1 mark

1 mark
• Tax paid at **20%** on **£37,000** (£300k – £263k) = **£7,400** (assuming the trustees pay the tax)

If the donor dies within seven years.

1 mark
• Death rate at date of death will apply to transfer

1 mark
• Tax is recalculated using the **value of gift at date of transfer and death nil rate band**

1 mark
• Taper relief is available to reduce the tax payable.

1 mark

Total: 6 marks
• Lifetime IHT already paid is treated as tax credit (subtracted) but cannot produce a repayment of lifetime tax

22 GILES

Giles must either:

2 marks
• have owned the farm and occupied it himself for agricultural purposes for at least two years before the transfer; or

2 marks

Total: 4 marks
• have owned the farm for seven years before the transfer during which it was occupied either by himself or someone else for agricultural purposes.

23 GREGORY

1 mark
The gift of the house to Ronald by Gregory is a gift with reservation of benefit.

1 mark
This is because Gregory continues to live in the house by himself without paying full consideration.

1 mark
When the gift was made, this was still a potentially exempt transfer of the value of the house at this time.

1 mark
The value of the house is also included in Gregory's estate at the date of his death.

1 mark
Since this gives a double charge to tax on the same property, only the charge which gives the higher tax total will be charged, not both.

Total: 5 marks

24 DEATH ESTATE

1 mark
The variation must be made by the beneficiary varying his entitlement, who must be over the age of eighteen and sane.

1 mark
The variation must be made for no consideration.

1 mark
It must be made in writing.

1 mark
It must be made within two years of death.

2 marks

Total: 6 marks
A statement must be included in the variation that the will is to be treated as rewritten. The statement is made by the beneficiary and also the personal representatives of the estate if more IHT becomes payable.

25 JOHN

	£	
Proceeds on encashment	20,000	
Add: early withdrawals 5 × 4% × £15,000	3,000	*1 mark*
	23,000	
Less: initial premium	(15,000)	*1 mark*
Overall profit	8,000	*1 mark*
Number of complete years is 5 so slice is £8,000 ÷ 5 =	£1,600	*1 mark*

Basic rate band remaining
1 mark

  £(31,400 – 30,200) = £1,200

Additional tax on slice

  £(1,600 – 1,200) = 400 × 18% = £72
1 mark
1 mark

Tax on bond £72 × 5 = £360
Total: 7 marks

26 ISA

A 'mini' individual savings account (ISA) consists of one component out of cash, life assurance and 'stocks and shares'.
1 mark

A 'maxi' ISA must include a stocks and shares component and may also offer cash and/or life assurance components.
1 mark

Three separate mini ISAs (one for each component) may be taken out during each tax year, or one maxi ISA, but it is not possible to take out both a mini and maxi ISA in the same tax year.
1 mark

The limits for an investor aged 18 or over are:

	Maxi £	Mini £	
Cash	3,000	3,000	*1 mark*
Life assurance	1,000	1,000	*1 mark*
Stocks and shares		3,000	*1 mark*
balance up to	7,000		*1 mark*

Total: 7 marks

27 PENELOPE

- The letting must be of furnished accommodation in the UK
1 mark

- It must be made on a commercial basis with a view to realisation of profit
1 mark

- It must be available for commercial letting to the public for not less than 140 days in a year and actually let for at least 70 days in that 140 day period (average if two or more properties)
2 mark

- For at least 7 months (including the 70 days) it is not normally in the same occupation for more than 31 days.
1 mark

Total: 5 marks

28 MR TIPPETT

Basis year for 2004/05 can be any year from 1999/00 to 2004/05.
1 mark

Basis year should be 1999/00 as this has highest NRE (£38,000) in the period
1 mark

Age at beginning of year of payment is 41
1 mark

Percentage of NRE is therefore 20%
1 mark

Maximum contribution is 20% × £38,000 = £7,600
1 mark

Total: 5 marks

29 ENTERPRISE INVESTMENT SCHEME

1 mark

1 mark

1 mark

1 mark

Total: 4 marks

Income tax relief of 20% on amount invested up to £200,000 provided investment maintained for 3 years.

No **CGT on disposal** after **3 years**

A CGT gain may be **deferred by re-investment** into EIS provided the investment is made one year before/within three years after disposal

30 URSULA

(a) Three examples of investments which need to be converted

2 marks

(i) Offshore roll-up fund because no income would be produced which would disadvantage the income beneficiary.

2 marks

(ii) High coupon gilt because there would be little chance of growth and this would disadvantage the capital beneficiary.

2 marks

(iii) Royalties as these would produce income but the capital value would reduce to nil on the expiry date and therefore would disadvantage the capital beneficiary.

Total: 6 marks

(*Note*. Marks are given for alternative valid examples.)

1 mark

(b) The trustees have a duty to convert as soon as possible.

1 mark

Total: 2 marks

Since there is no power to postpone conversion, the trustees should convert within one year of the death of the settlor.

31 CERTAINTIES

The case of *Knight v Knight* (1840) set out the certainties required for a trust to be valid:

1 mark

(a) certainty of words used

2 marks

(b) certainty of subject matter (trust property and beneficiaries' interests)

1 mark

(c) certainty of objects (beneficiaries)

Total: 4 marks

Tutor's comments

Learn these three 'certainties' – they are often tested in short questions or part of a 40 mark question.

32 TRUSTEES

(a) Five persons who may appoint trustees are:

1 mark

(i) the settlor/testator in the case of initial trustees

1 mark

(ii) a court if no trustees are appointed or where there are no persons available to appoint trustees

1 mark

(iii) beneficiaries in certain cases under the Trusts of Land and Appointment of Trustees Act 1996

1 mark

(iv) a person specified in the trust as having the power to appoint trustees

1 mark

(v) the surviving trustees, or, if none, the personal representatives of the longest surviving trustee

Total: 5 marks

1 mark

(b) The maximum number of trustees of a trust of land is four.

33 BENEFICIARIES

Two advantages of using the Married Woman's Property Act 1882 *1 mark*

(a) Simplicity and the certainty of beneficiaries *1 mark*

(b) Good protection from creditors

Two disadvantages *1 mark*

(a) Restriction on who can be beneficiaries *1 mark*

(b) Own life policies only *Total: 4 marks*

34 LOUISA

Louisa would receive Wesley's personal chattels and a legacy of £125,000 under the rules of *1 mark*
intestacy and also the house held as joint tenants by survivorship.

The residue of the estate would be: *1 mark*

	£
Bank a/c (1/2 shares)	5,000
Quoted investments	85,000
Life assurance policy proceeds	300,000	*1 mark*
	390,000
Less: legacy to Louisa	(125,000)
Residue	265,000	*1 mark*

Of this half (£132,500) would be held on trust for Louisa for life. On her death, the trust *2 marks*
would be held equally for the children.

Of the other half, £66,250 would pass immediately to Emma and the other £66,250 would be *2 marks*
held in trust for Sarah until she attained the age of 18 years.

Total: 8 marks

Tutor's comments

This is the commonest division of an estate on intestacy. Notice the difference between
holding assets as joint tenants (automatic accrual to survivor) and tenants in common
(deceased's share passes under intestacy (or will if one had been made)). You need to be
accurate about the figures involved.

35 SALLY SMITH

(a) The policy must be on a single life basis. *1 mark*

The policy must be expressed to be for the benefit of their spouse (and children). *1 mark*

The beneficiaries can be listed by name, or described by relationship. *1 mark*

The policy is written in trust from the outset. *1 mark*

Total: 4 marks

(b) The sum assured is protected even if the policy was taken out with the intent to
defraud creditors. *1 mark*

The most that the trustee in bankruptcy can claim are the premiums paid if it can be *1 mark*
proved that the policy was taken out with the intention of defrauding creditors.

Total: 2 marks

36 ACCUMULATION PERIODS

1 mark

Under the Law of Property Act 1925, income can be accumulated for one of the following periods:

1 mark

- Life of the settlor

1 mark

- 21 years after the death of the settlor

1 mark

- Minority of any persons living at the death of the settlor

1 mark

- Minority of any beneficiaries who would be entitled to have their share of income accumulated after attaining majority

1 mark

- 21 years from the date of the settlement

Total: 6 marks

- Minority of any person in being out at the date of settlement.

37 TAX PLANNING

The main tax planning considerations are:

1 mark

(a) the transfer of assets into the trust will be a potentially exempt transfer (PET).

1 mark

(b) the transfer of chargeable assets into the trust will be a disposal for CGT.

2 marks

(c) the child beneficiary is liable to any CGT, but their annual exemption will be available and rates of tax will be used.

2 marks

(d) all the income of the trust will be taxed on the parent unless it does not exceed £100.

Total: 6 marks

Tutor's comments

You must discuss the three personal taxes, IT, CGT and IHT in a question on tax planning. Note the rules about IT on bare trusts set up by a parent.

38 G TRUST

Income tax computation: 2004/05

	Non-savings Income	Savings Income (gross)
	£	£
Schedule A (5,900 – 780)	5,120	
Debenture interest received $2,320 \times \frac{100}{80}$		2,900
Less: Trust expenses $300 \times \frac{100}{80}$		(375)
Gross income liable to trust rate tax	5,120	2,525
Tax payable under self assessment		
375 @ 20%	75	
5,120 + 2,525 @ 40%	3,058	
Less: tax suffered (2,900 @ 20%)	(580)	
	2,553	

1 mark (Schedule A)

1 mark (Debenture interest)

1 mark (Less: Trust expenses)

1 mark (375 @ 20%)

1 mark (5,120 + 2,525 @ 40%)

1 mark

1 mark

R185	Gross	Tax	Net
	£	£	£
	1,667	667	1,000
		(1,000 × 40/60)	

Total: 7 marks

39   **SETTLOR**

The settlor could set up an accumulation and maintenance trust under which the beneficiaries must become entitled to at least the right to income at an age not exceeding 25 years, but need not become entitled to capital.   *1 mark*

The creation of the trust would be a potentially exempt transfer (PET).   *1 mark*

The transfer of the shares to the trust would be a disposal for CGT and there would be no gift relief available.   *1 mark*

The settlor could alternatively set up a discretionary trust under which the beneficiaries will not be entitled to income or capital.   *1 mark*

The creation of the trust would be a chargeable lifetime transfer, but no tax would be payable as the amount of the transfer would be within the nil band.   *1 mark*

The transfer of the shares to the trust would be a disposal for CGT and there would be gift relief available because there is a charge to IHT.   *1 mark*

Total: 6 marks

Tutor's comments

You may have thought that gift relief was not available on the gift to the discretionary trust because there was no IHT payable. The condition for gift relief being available is that there is a *charge* to IHT, even if this is at 0%.

40   **BILL**

(a)   An interest in possession has at least one beneficiary who is entitled to the income from the trust.   *1 mark*

A discretionary trust has no such beneficiary.   *1 mark*

None of the beneficiaries are entitled to anything until the trustees exercise their discretion.   *1 mark*
Total: 3 marks

(b)   The transfer in would be a PET for IHT purposes.   *1 mark*

No IHT would be payable providing Bill survived for 7 years.   *1 mark*

The change of ownership is a CGT disposal.   *1 mark*

Bill will be liable to pay CGT at his marginal rate, as gift relief not available.   *1 mark*
Total: 4 marks

(c)   •   The transfer in would be a chargeable lifetime transfer for IHT purposes.   *1 mark*

   •   Tax would be payable if the cumulative value of chargeable transfers exceed the nil rate band.   *1 mark*

   •   Any CGT due in respect of the change of ownership can be held over.   *1 mark*

   •   The gain would effectively be chargeable on the trustees and not Bill on a later disposal.   *1 mark*
Total: 4 marks

41   **BARE TRUST**

(a)   A bare trust is one where the trustees hold property on behalf of someone who is **absolutely entitled** to that property (or would be if he were not a minor).   *1 mark*

The sole duty of the trustee is **to hold the property for the beneficiary** and transfer it to him when required.   *1 mark*
Total: 2 marks

(b)   •   The trustees have no liability for income tax.   *1 mark*
   •   Income is assessed on the parent.   *1 mark*
   Unless it is < £100 pa   *1 mark*
Total: 3 marks

42 DEATH BENEFITS

Any four of the following benefits:

1 mark

(a) The member can nominate the beneficiary of any death benefit.

1 mark

(b) The member can change the nominated beneficiaries according to changing circumstances.

1 mark

(c) There is no delay in death benefits being paid out as the benefit passes outside the deceased's estate and is therefore not subject to probate.

1 mark

(d) As the death benefit passes outside the estate, there is no IHT payable on it.

1 mark
Total: 4 marks

(e) The beneficiary could be a further trust, eg a discretionary trust created in the member's lifetime.

43 VOLUNTARY ARRANGEMENT

1 mark

An individual voluntary arrangement is an arrangement between a debtor in financial difficulty and his creditors.

2 marks

It is usually made in an attempt to avoid a bankruptcy order, to avoid the disgrace of bankruptcy and disabilities associated with it eg inability to be a company director.

1 mark

It is advantageous for the creditors because they are likely to receive a higher proportion of the money owned to them and sooner.

1 mark
Total: 5 marks

The costs of bankruptcy proceedings are higher than for a voluntary agreement.

44 POWER OF ATTORNEY

1 mark

(a) A power of attorney is made by a person ('the donor').

1 mark

It appoints another person ('the attorney' or 'the donee').

1 mark

The donee is appointed to act for the donor in legal matters eg to sign documents on behalf of the donor.

1 mark

(b) The general power of attorney under s10 Powers of Attorney Act 1971 first sets out the names of the donor and the donee.

1 mark

It states that the donee is appointed as attorney for the donor.

1 mark
Total: 6 marks

The document must be executed as a deed.

45 ELSIE

1 mark

(a) Enduring power of attorney (EPA)

1 mark

(b) Dorothy must apply to the Public Trustee Office to have the EPA registered if Elsie is (or is becoming) mentally incapable.

1 mark

She must give notice to Elsie and at least 3 close relatives.

1 mark

Until application, Dorothy cannot use the EPA.

1 mark

After application, Dorothy has limited powers (eg to maintain Elsie) until registration.

2 mark
Total: 7 marks

After registration, Dorothy can make binding decisions about Elsie's property within the limits of the Enduring Powers of Attorney Act 1985.

46   MR K

(a)   MR K'S BENEFITS

		£	
Jaguar:	car $20,000 \times 28\% \times \dfrac{4}{12}$ (W1)	1,867	*3 marks*
	fuel $14,400 \times 28\% \times 4/12$ (partial reimbursement not effective)	1,344	*3 marks*
Mercedes:	no private use	-	*1 mark*
BMW:	car $15,000 \times 29\%$ (W2)	4,350	*3 marks*
	fuel $14,400 \times 29\%$	4,176	*2 marks*
Total car and fuel benefits		11,737	*1 mark*
Legal costs		2,000	*1 mark*
Use of suits £800 × 20%		160	*1 mark*
Total benefits		13,897	*Total: 15 marks*

Workings

(W1)   (210 – 145) = 65 ÷ 5 = 13 plus basic % (15) = 28%
(W2)   (215 – 145) = 70 ÷ 5 = 14 plus basic % (15) = 29%

(b)   MR K'S TAX LIABILITY

	Non-savings income	*Dividend income*	*Total income*	
	£	£	£	*1 mark*
Salary	43,484		43,484	*1 mark*
Benefits	13,897		13,897	*1 mark*
Dividends £18,000 × 100/80		20,000	20,000	*2 marks*
STI	57,381	20,000	77,381	*2 marks*
Less: PA	(4,745)	(-)	(4,745)	*1 mark*
Taxable income	52,636	20,000	72,636	*2 marks*

Tax liability

	£	
£2,020 @ 10%	202	*1 mark*
£29,380 @ 22%	6,464	*1 mark*
£(52,636 – 31,400) = 21,236 @ 40%	8,494	*2 marks*
£20,000 @ 32½%	6,500	*2 marks*
Total tax liability	21,660	*1 mark*
		2 marks
		1 mark

(c)   Mr K's payment under self assessment

Total: 20 marks

	£	
Total tax liability as (b)	21,660	*1 mark*
Less: PAYE	(14,511)	*1 mark*
Tax credit on dividends £20,000 × 10%	(2,000)	*1 mark*
Tax payable under self assessment	5,149	*1 mark*
Due 31.1.2006		*1 mark*

Tutor's comments

Total: 5 marks

Basic income tax computations are an important part of the exam. Make sure you know the pro-forma, especially the split between non-savings, savings (other than dividends) income and dividend income. Dividend income is taxed as the highest part of income and at 32½% rather than 40%.

Learn the self assessment payment date – it's an easy mark.

47   JIM SMITH

(a)

	Non-savings £	Savings £	Dividends £
Salary	35,000		
Car benefit: £11,110 × 30% (W)	3,333		
Less pension contributions	(1,750)		
Building Society Interest: £700 × 100/80 × ½		437	
Unit Trust Dividends: £250 × 100/80 *(interest distribution)*		313	
Share Dividends: £360 × 100/90			400
STI	36,583	750	400
Less personal allowance	(4,745)		
Taxable Income	31,838	750	400

1 mark
2 mark
1 mark
1 mark

1 mark
1 mark

1 mark

	£
Non-Savings income	
2,020 @ 10%	202
29,380 @ 22%	6,464
438 @ 40%	175
31,838	
Savings income	
437 + 313 = 750 @ 40%	300
Dividends	
400 @ 32.5%	130
	7,271
Less: EIS relief @ 20%	(2,000)
Income tax liability	5,271
⇒ Income after tax and pension contributions	
= 34,400* – 5,271 =	28,939

1 mark
1 mark
1 mark

1 mark

1 mark
1 mark
1 mark

1 marks
1 mark

2 marks Total: 19 marks

* (35,000 – 1,750 + 437 + 313 + 400)

Working

(220 – 145) = 75 ÷ 5 = 15 + basic % (15) = 30%

(b)

On first £395.00	=		NIL
9.4% on £2,248 (£2,643 – £395)	=		£211.31
1% on £274 (£2,917 – £2,643)			£2.74
Rebate 1.6% on £395 – £342			£0.85
Total NIC	£(211.31 + 2.74 – 0.85) × 12 =		£2,558.40

2 marks
2 marks
2 marks
1 mark
1 mark
Total: 8 marks

(c) He could transfer his share of Building Society deposit to wife.
She would pay tax at 20% only.
He could transfer shares & unit trust to wife.
She will pay tax at only 10%/20%.

1 mark
1 mark
1 mark
1 mark
Total: 4 marks

(d) He can transfer shares/Unit Trusts to wife.

Treated as passing across on a no gain/no loss basis.

Recipient acquires at spouse's base cost plus indexation.

She can then apply her own CGT allowance.

'Bed and breakfasting' is not possible without some investment risk being incurred.

He would need to sell the shares and buy back after 30 days later in order to crystallise gains for use of annual exemption.

1 mark
2 marks
1 mark
1 mark
2 marks
2 marks
Total: 9 marks

Tutor's comment

If you know the income tax proforma, part (a) should have yielded good marks.

Part (b) was easy if you knew where to look in the Tax Tables.

The tax planning points in (c) and (d) should be noted.

48   ANDY

(a)   ESTATE, DATE OF DEATH 25 SEPTEMBER 2004

	£	£	
Free realty			
Freehold house		212,500	1 mark
Free personality			
Personal chattels		39,500	1 mark
Shares:			
COSA plc 25,000 at 31		7,750	2 marks
GA plc 10,000 at 112.5		11,250	2 marks
ADA plc 6,000 at 236.25		14,175	2 marks
Loan stock:			
18,000 at 68		12,240	1 mark
15,000 at 92		13,800	1 mark
Add: (15,000 × 8% × 1/2 less			
income tax at 20%)		480	1 mark
Cash in bank		53,797	1 mark
Unit trust 1,000 at 73		730	1 mark
Life assurance policy		9,000	1 mark
Buzzard Limited			3 marks
40/75 × 100,000 = £53,333		53,333	
(as £53,333 is higher than £30,000)			
Accrued interest on mother's fund			
(400 less 20% IT)		320	2 marks
Reversionary interest - exempt			1 mark
Less: reasonable funeral expenses (not mausoleum)		(816)	2 marks
		428,059	2 marks
Settled property			1 mark
Mother's fund (40,000 – 400)	39,600		1 mark
Father's fund ($^1/_2$ × 25,000)	12,500		1 mark
		52,100	1 mark
Chargeable estate		480,159	

Total: 28 marks

(b)   IHT LIABILITY ON DEATH

Lifetime gift – PET now charged ie

Gift	74,000	1 mark
Less: ME	(1,000)	1 mark
AE 2003/04	(3,000)	1 mark
AE 2002/03 b/f	(3,000)	1 mark
Transfer of value	67,000	

Within nil band – no IHT payable   1 mark

Death estate (as above)   480,159

1 mark

Nil rate band remaining £(263,000 – 67,000) = £196,000

1 mark

Tax @ 40% on £(480,159 – 196,000) = £284,159 is £113,664   2 marks

Total: 9 marks

(c)

		£
	Trustees of mother's fund	
1 mark	$\dfrac{39,600}{480,159} \times £113,664 =$	9,374
	Trustees of father's fund	
1 mark	$\dfrac{12,500}{480,159} \times £113,664 =$	2,959
	PRs	
1 mark	$\dfrac{428,059}{480,159} \times £113,664 =$	101,331

Total: 3 marks

Tutor's comments

Basic IHT computations are important and lead to the basis of planning advice. Watch out for the division into free estate/settled property and notice the effect on allocation of tax. On related property, remember that Andy is not treated as owing 7,500 shares, but a proportion of the value of 7,500 shares.

49   HAWKSBILL

(a)   IHT on lifetime gift

		£
1 mark	CLT (7.00)	255,600
1 mark	00/01 AE	(3,000)
1 mark	99/00 AE B/F	(3,000)
		249,600
2 marks	IHT payable by Hawksbill $(249,600 - 234,000) \times \dfrac{20}{80}$	3,900
1 mark	Gross transfer = 249,600 + 3,900 = £253,500	

1 mark
1 mark

Death tax

	CLT (7.00)	253,500
	(covered by 263k nil band)	

Total: 8 marks

(b) IHT on estate

Estate	£	£	
Free estate			
X plc shares: 0.25			
20,000 @ 166.25p (W1)		33,250	*4 marks*
Y plc shares			
6,000 @ lower of 80.25p/81p			*2 marks*
ie 6,000 × 80.25p	4,815		
Add: dividend			*1 mark*
6,000 × 5p	300		
		5,115	
		38,365	
Family company (W2)		9,697	*4 marks*
Bank balances		16,400	*1 mark*
Freehold property	300,000		*1 mark*
Less: mortgage	(85,000)		*1 mark*
		215,000	
Villa in Spain		59,850	
Less: Debts and liabilities	1,340		*1 mark*
CGT	3,920		*1 mark*
Funeral	3,870		*1 mark*
		(9,130)	*1 mark*
Net free estate		330,182	*1 mark*
Settled property			
Life tenancy	58,300		*1 mark*
Reversionary interest	-		*1 mark*
(excluded property)		58,300	*1 mark*
Total chargeable estate		388,482	*1 mark*
			1 mark

Nil rate band available

£(263,000 – 253,500) = £9,500   *1 mark*

IHT on estate

	£	
		1 mark
Gross IHT = 9,500 @ nil		*1 mark*
378,982 @ 40% =	151,593	
388,482		
Less: QSR (W3)	(2,128)	*3 marks*
	149,465	
		1 mark

Estate rate: 149,465/388,482 = 38.47411%

IHT on free estate, payable by executors		
330,182 × 38.47411%	127,035	
IHT settled property, payable by trustees:		
58,300 × 38.47411%	22,430	*1 mark*

Total: 32 marks

Workings

(W1) X plc shares

Valued at lowest of:

7.6.04	¼ up	166.25p	(lowest)
	mid bargain	167.5p	
10.6.04	¼ up	167.5p	
	mid bargain	168p	

(W2) Family company

At death, shares would be valued using related property rules:

	£
$\frac{4{,}000}{4{,}000+1{,}000+500} \times 80{,}000 =$	58,182

BPR would be available at 100%, but restricted for the excepted asset (land):

	£
Value at death	58,182
Less: BPR 100% × 58,182 × $\frac{150}{180}$	(48,485)
	9,697

(W3) Quick succession relief

$$80\% \times 2{,}960 \times \frac{(29{,}200 - 2{,}960)}{29{,}200} = \text{£}2{,}128$$

QSR reduces the estate rate and is not just a credit for the IHT on the trust.

Tutor's Comments

Remember that IHT is concerned with 'loss to donor', so if the donor pays the IHT on a CLT, you need to gross up. Watch out for restriction on BPR for assets not used in business – it frequently turns up in questions.

50 KEN SING

(a) Ken is **not domiciled** in the UK, so his **foreign income and gains are only taxable in the UK to the extent that they are remitted** to the UK. On the other hand, interest and dividends taxable on the remittance basis are *non-savings* income.

KEN SING: INCOME TAX COMPUTATION

		Non-savings	*Savings*	*Dividend*	*Total*
		£	£	£	£
1 mark	Salary	75,765			
1 mark	Car benefit £38,000 × 30% (W)	11,400			
1 mark	Fuel benefit £14,400 × 30%	4,320			
1 mark	Cheap taxable loan £90,000 × 5%	4,500			
1 mark	Medical insurance	1,200			
	Golf club subscription	1,500			
	Earnings	98,185			
	Schedule D Case V				
1 mark	Rents £3,500 × 100/70	5,000			
1 mark	Interest £850 × 100/85	1,000			
1 mark	UK dividends 100,000 × 9p × 100/90			10,000	
1 mark	UK bank interest £2,240 × 100/80		2,800		
	STI	104,185	2,800	10,000	116,985
	Less personal allowance	(4,745)			(4,745)
	Taxable income	99,440	2,800	10,000	112,240

Working

(220 – 145) = 75 ÷ 5 = 15 + basic % (15) = 30%

Income tax

£2,020 × 10%		202	*1 mark*
£29,380 × 22%		6,464	*1 mark*
£70,840 × 40%		28,336	*1 mark*
£10,000 × 32.5%		3,250	*1 mark*
		38,252	

Less double taxation relief (foreign tax lower than UK)			*1 mark*
Rents £5,000 × 30%	1,500		
Interest £1,000 × 15%	150		
		(1,650)	*1 mark*
Tax liability		36,602	
Less tax suffered and tax credits			
PAYE	34,273		
Dividends £10,000 × 10%	1,000		
Interest £2,800 × 20%	560		
		(35,833)	*1 mark*
Tax payable		769	

KEN SING: CGT COMPUTATION

		£	
Sale of land in Pajan			
Proceeds		40,000	
Less cost £50,000 × 40/(40 + 120)		(12,500)	*1 mark*
		27,500	
Less indexation allowance			
0.752 × £12,500		(9,400)	*1 mark*
Indexed gain		18,100	
Gain after taper relief (6.4.98 - 5.4.04 = 6 years plus additional year			*1 mark*
= 7 years) 75% × £18,100		13,575	
Less annual exemption		(8,200)	
Taxable gain		5,375	*1 mark*

CGT: £5,375 × 40% = £2,150.

Total: 20 marks

Ignore the sale of paintings because the proceeds have not been remitted to the UK.

(b) KEN SING: INHERITANCE TAX COMPUTATION

Because Ken Sing is not UK domiciled, his overseas assets are excluded property. Land and buildings are situated at their physical location, shares where registered and bank accounts where the relevant branches are located. *1 mark*

	£	£	
House in London £(178,000 – 90,000)		88,000	*1 mark*
Bank account in England		76,000	*1 mark*
UK shares: 100,000 × £1.04		104,000	*1 mark*
UK shares	65,000		*1 mark*
Less BPR £65,000 × 250/262.5 × 100%	(61,905)		*1 mark*
		3,095	
		271,095	
		£	

Inheritance tax			
£263,000 × 0%		0	*1 mark*
£8,095 × 40%		3,238	*1 mark*
271,095		3,238	
Less quick succession relief			
£13,333 × $\dfrac{45,000}{58,333}$ × 20% (4 to 5 years)		(2,057)	*1 marks*
		1,181	

Total: 10 marks

(c)   KEN SING: REVISED CGT COMPUTATION FOR 2005/06

1 mark

The London house appears to have been Ken Sing's principal private residence throughout, so any gain or loss will be ignored.

The gain on the shares in High Growth plc is as follows.

	£
1 mark Proceeds 100,000 × £1.02	102,000
Less cost	(45,000)
1 mark Gain	57,000
Gain after taper relief (Sept 2000 – Sept 2004 = 4 years 90% × £57,000	51,300

The gain on the shares in Small-time Ltd is as follows.

	£
1 mark Proceeds	65,000
Less cost	(20,000)
1 mark Unindexed gain	45,000
Less indexation	(2,918)
Indexed gain	42,082

1 mark

Gain after taper relief (6.4.98 - 5.4.05 = 7 years) 25% × £42,082 =	10,520

The shares in Small Time Ltd are business assets pre 6.4.00 (at least 25% holding) and afterwards.

The final computation is as follows.

	£
Gain on High-Growth plc shares	51,300
Gain on Small-time plc shares	10,520
Chargeable gains	61,820
Less annual exemption	(8,200)
1 mark Taxable gains	53,620
1 mark CGT £53,620 × 40%	21,448

1 mark

Ken Sing is permanently leaving the UK. This means that he should not be caught by the anti-avoidance rules applicable to temporary non-residence.

1 mark

Sales after returning to Pajan will therefore be exempt from CGT, so long as the Revenue treat Ken Sing as no longer UK resident nor ordinary resident. The Revenue must so treat him from 6 April 2005.

Total: 10 marks

Tutor's comments

There is usually a question in the exam requiring calculation of income tax on various sources of income, so you need to be able to set out the pro-forma quickly.

Note the point about the foreign income being non-savings income. However, this was not actually important in this question because the income was clearly all taxable at 40%.

Where there is a part disposal of an asset (usually land), the cost of the part disposed of is:

$$\frac{A}{A+B} \text{ where}$$

A is the proceeds of the part sold and B is the market value of the remaining part.

A person who is not UK domiciled is only liable to IHT on UK assets. Most of the situs rules are fairly obvious eg house in London situated in UK. The bank account 'branch' rule should be noted.

You must be able to spot when taper relief applies and what type of asset (business/non-business) is involved.

Watch out for the rule that non-residents are not generally liable to CGT, even on UK situate assets. Resident, but non-domiciled, individuals are liable on a remittance basis on non-UK gains and on an arising basis for UK gains.

51   SEBASTIAN WORTH

(a)   IHT on lifetime gifts

December 1998 gifts

(i)   The gifts to the nephews are each covered by the 'small gifts' exemption.   *1 mark*

(ii)   The gift of £83,000 to the friend is a PET.   *1 mark*
       Tax only arises if donor dies within 7 years.   *1 mark*
       When this happens, the amount chargeable is

	83,000
98/99 AE	(3,000)
97/98 AE	(3,000)
	77,000

1 mark

This will be taxed @ 40% due to the fact that the two previous CLT's within the immediately preceding 7 years exceed £263,000 in total.   *1 mark*

ie IHT on death = £30,800   *1 mark*

Tapered to £12,320 (survived 5-6 years)   *1 mark* *1 mark*

Payable by friend

February 2001 gift

This is a CLT, subject to lifetime IHT when the gift is made.   *1 mark*

No nil band due to level of earlier CLT's.   *1 mark*

As Sebastian pays the tax, the amount put in the trust is a *net* transfer and the tax rate is ¼ of the net.   *1 mark*

ie	58,000
00/01 AE	(3,000)
99/00 AE	(3,000)
	52,000 × ¼ = £13,000 IHT

1 mark
1 mark

⇒ Gross chargeable transfer = 52K + 13K = £65,000

When the death occurs, the tax is calculated as:

65,000 @ 40% =	26,000
Tapered to	20,800 (80%)
Less: L/T tax	(13,000)
Death tax	7,800 *payable by trustees*

1 mark
1 mark
1 mark
1 mark

March 2004 gift

This is a PET which becomes chargeable to death tax.   *1 mark* *1 mark*

However, it will be covered by 100% business property relief as the son still owns at the date of Sebastian's death.   *1 mark*

IHT due on estate

		£
1 mark	Estate	
1 mark	Assets	274,000
1 mark	Less: debts etc	(3,780)
	Guarantee	(6,000)
		264,220
	Less: left to wife	(60,000)
	Chargeable	204,220
	Nil band	263,000
	Less: Transfers in previous 7 years	
	7.12.98	(77,000)
	3.2.01	(65,000)
	Remaining nil band	121,000
	121,000 @ Nil	
	83,220 @ 40% =	33,288 payable by executors
	204,220	

1 mark

Total: 24 marks

1 mark

(b) It is possible to alter a will by a deed of variation.

The conditions for a deed of variation to be effective for inheritance tax purposes are as follows.

2 marks

(i) The variation must be made in writing by those who benefit or would have benefited under the dispositions concerned within two years of the death.

1 mark

(ii) The variation must include a statement that the will is to be treated as rewritten by the variation.

1 mark

(iii) The variation must not be made for a consideration other than another variation or disclaimer of a disposition forming part of the same estate.

Sebastian has wasted his business property relief as he left the relevant asset it to his wife.

1 mark

Any assets left to his wife are automatically exempt, therefore he should have left other

1 mark

assets worth £120,000 to his wife.

1 mark

Total: 8 marks

The business should have been left specifically to Emma so as to use the 100% BPR on it.

(c) In order to be liable to UK capital gains tax on gains arising in a year of assessment the

1 mark

person to whom the gain accrues must be either resident or ordinarily resident in the UK in the year of assessment.

1 mark

Where a person leaves the UK, having been resident for at least 4 of the last 7 years:

1 mark

(i) Any gains realised in the whole year of departure are assessable, and

2 marks

(ii) If the person becomes resident again, having been not resident and not ordinarily resident for less than 5 complete tax years, any gains made on assets held at date of departure from the UK will be assessable in the year of return.

2 marks

However, gains arising to a non resident and non ordinarily resident person on an asset located in the UK will be chargeable if the person is carrying on a trade through a branch or agency and the asset is used in the trade or otherwise held for the purposes of the branch or agency.

1 mark

Total: 8 marks

Domicile status is of importance where gains are realised on overseas assets. Whereas a person resident or ordinarily resident in the UK is liable on gains arising on his assets wherever located, a person with non UK domicile is only chargeable on overseas gains if the proceeds are remitted to the UK.

52   LEN SHACKLETON

(a)   In October 2004 transfer is a PET and no IHT liability arises at that time.

2 marks

In May 2007 transfer is a CLT giving rise to IHT at half the death rates.

£

270,000	
(263,000) @ 0%	Nil
7,000 @ 20%	1,400
	1,400

On death the PET will affect the death computation.

1.10.04 transfer	275,000	
	(263,000)	
	12,000 @ 40%	4,800

Tapered to 2,880 (40% relief)

2.5.07 transfer £270,000 @ 40%*	108,000
Less lifetime IHT paid	(1,400)
	106,600

2.6.09 death Estate 600,000 @ 40%	240,000

* No nil band due to earlier PET becoming chargeable.

(b) (i)   Raich can effect a Deed of Variation

(ii)   • If Raich becomes entitled to property under a will he can vary his entitlement

• Such a variation is not treated as a transfer of value by Raich of the conditions are complied with

• The inheritance can be made to 'skip' a generation without any IHT being paid

(iii)   The following conditions must apply.

• The variation must be executed within 2 years of death and must include a statement that the will is to be rewritten in the terms of the variation.

• The variation must be in writing.

• It must be signed by the person who would have benefited.

• No payment or consideration may pass between beneficiaries in order to induce them to enter into a variation.

(c) (i)   • Gift Inter Vivos 7 year reducing balance term policy for PET for the benefit of Charlie

(ii)   • Whole of life policy in flexible trust for the benefit of Raich and Billy in equal shares as default beneficiaries

Tutor's comment

Learn the conditions for an effective variation of a will – this is often examined.

The use of life policies to cover IHT liabilities is an important exam area.

2 marks
2 marks
1 mark
1 mark
1 mark
1 mark
1 mark
2 marks
2 marks
2 marks
1 mark
1 mark
2 marks
1 mark
Total: 20 marks
2 marks
1 mark
2 marks
1 mark
1 mark
Total: 5 marks
1 mark
2 marks
1 mark
1 mark
2 marks
Total: 7 marks
2 marks
1 mark
Total: 3 marks
2 marks
1 mark
Total: 3 marks

53 TANNIA WHITING

(a) 2004/2005 income tax computation

		Non savings income £	Savings income £	Dividend income £
1 mark	Schedule DI	40,500		
1 mark	Local authority bond £240 x 100/80		300	
1 mark	Unit trust dividend £2,700 x 100/90			3,000
1 mark	STI	40,500	300	3,000
1 mark	Less: PA	(4,745)		
	Taxable income	35,755	300	3,000

Tax

		£
1 mark	£2,020 @ 10%	202
1 mark	£29,380 @ 22%	6,464
	£3,077 @ 22% (W1)	677
	£34,477	
2 marks	£(35,755 – 34,477 + 300) = 1,578 @ 40%	631
1 mark	£3,000 @ 32.5%	975
1 mark	Tax liability	8,949
1 mark	Less: on a/c (W2)	(8,429)
1 mark	bond tax at source	(60)
1 mark	dividend credit	(300)
	Tax now payable	160

Workings

1. Basic rate band extension for pension payments

   3 marks £200 × 100/78 × 12 = £3,077

2. Payments on account for 2004/05 half of 2003/04 tax assessable which was:

			Non savings Income £
1 mark	Schedule DI/STI		40,000
1 mark	Less: PA		(4,615)
1 mark	Taxable income		35,385
	Tax		
1 mark	£1,960 @ 10%		196
1 mark	£28,540 @ 22%		6,279
1 mark	£4,885 @ 40%		1,954
			8,429
1 mark	Paid on a/c	31.1.05	4,214
1 mark		31.7.05	4,215

Total: 25 marks

(b) *1 mark* Tannia can choose any of the three years 2002/03, 2003/04 or 2004/05 as the basis year.

1 mark She should choose 2004/05 as this gives the highest net relevant earnings.

1 mark Tannia is aged 42 at the beginning of 2004/05.

1 mark The maximum contribution that she can make is therefore 20% x £45,000 = £8,100 (gross).

She has already made contributions of £3,077 so the balance is £5,023. *1 mark*

This is a net contribution of £5,023 × 78/100 of £3,918. *1 mark*

The contribution must be made by 31 January 2006. *1 mark*

An election to carry back the contribution must be made at the same time or before the contribution is made. *1 mark*
2 marks

The basic rate band for 2004/05 will be extended by a further £5,023, making all of the taxable income below the basic rate band limit. *Total: 10 marks*

Note. The rules covering pensions will be replaced with effect from 6 April 2006. The key feature of the new regime will be an overall lifetime allowance for pension savings. Transitional rules will apply to rights accrued at 5 April 2006.

(c) The legacy of £2,500 should be invested in a cash ISA (Adam is aged 17). *1 mark*
1 mark

This can be a mini-ISA or a maxi-ISA with a cash only component. *1 mark*

The maximum amount of investment per tax year is £3,000, so Adam could top up the investment to this amount. *1 mark*

There will be no income tax on the interest earned by the ISA which is advantageous since Adam is a basic rate tax payer. *1 mark*

Adam will be able to withdraw the cash without any penalty next year. *Total: 5 marks*

54 SALLY AND GEORGE

(a) GEORGE

	Non-Savings income £	Savings income £	Dividend income £	
Pensions	17,400			*1 mark*
BSI (x 100/80)		375		*1 mark*
Dividends (x 100/90)			644	*1 mark*
Unit trust dividend				*3 marks*
(600 − 40) × 100/90			622	*1 mark*
PA	(4,745)	___	___	
	12,655	375	1,266	
2,020 @ 10% =		202		*1 mark*
<u>10,635</u> @ 22% =		2,340		*1 mark*
<u>12,665</u>				
375 @ 20%		75		*2 marks*
1,266 @ 10%		127		*2 marks*
		2,744		
Less: MCA (W)		(565)		*1 mark*
IT liability		2,179		

(W)	Age allowance available due to Sally's age.		*1 mark*
	His STI = 17,400 + 375 +1,266 =	19,041	*1 mark*
	Allowance available is:		
		5,725	
	Less: ½ (19,041 − 18,900) =	(71)	*3 marks*
		5,654	*1 mark*
			Total: 20 marks
	5,654 @ 10% =	565	

(b) SALLY

	Non-Savings income £	Savings income £	Dividend income £
Pension	1,060		
Pension	8,350		
Building Society 1100 × 100/80		1,375	
Dividends 750 × 100/90			833
SICAV Gain (no IA available)	1,500		
	10,910		
Less Personal Allowance	(6,830)		
Taxable income	4,080	1,375	833

1 mark
1 mark
1 mark
1 mark
2 marks

1 mark
3 marks
1 mark

No tax on corporate bond PEP

Tax payable:

Non-Savings income

	£
2,020 @ 10% =	202
2,060 @ 22% =	453
4,080	655
1,375 @ 20% =	275
833 @ 10% =	83
Total tax liability	1,013

1 mark
1 mark

1 mark
1 mark

Total: 15 marks

(c) Marginal rates of tax on investment income are the same.

Tax saving is related to age enhanced MCA.

George's Statutory total income would fall from £19,041 to £17,400 - below the threshold.

He would regain:

£71 @ 10% = £7

1 mark
1 mark
1 mark
2 marks
Total: 5 marks

Tutor's comment

The taxation of specific investments is often tested. Make sure you know the material in the Investments Chapter of your study text in detail. A general awareness is not enough.

55 **ROY AND CYBILLE**

(a) (i) A gift is made of the amount of the nil band available at the death of the testator, taking into account any previous lifetime gifts.

The gift is made into a discretionary trust.

The beneficiaries of the trust will include the surviving spouse and the grandchildren.

No IHT will be payable on the creation of the discretionary trust as, by definition, it is covered by the nil rate band.

If a capital distribution is made from the trust within two years, the distribution is treated as a direct gift under the deceased's will and there is no exit charge payable.

Any other capital distribution from the trust will be subject to an exit charge.

This would include the conversion of the trust to an accumulation and maintenance trust which might be appropriate after the death of the second spouse.

If the trust is still in existence ten years after the death, there will be a principal charge on it.

1 mark
1 mark
1 mark
1 mark
1 mark
1 mark
1 mark
1 mark
Total: 8 marks

(ii)   The nil rate band discretionary trust uses up the nil rate band which would otherwise be wasted if the whole estate of the first spouse to die passes to the other spouse.   *1 mark*

The circumstances at the time of the death of the first spouse can be taken into account when deciding how the estate is to pass.   *1 mark*

The discretionary trust avoids the 'bunching' of estates on the second death.   *1 mark*

The discretionary trust allows the spouse to benefit from the trust without the assets being in the estate of the spouse.   *1 mark*

The discretionary trust gives additional flexibility over the ultimate beneficiaries of the trust.   *1 mark*

The potential IHT saving is £263,000 × 40% = £105,200.   *1 mark*
Total: 6 marks

(iii)   The surviving spouse should be a beneficiary and trustee of the trust.   *1 mark*

The trustees should have to act unanimously.   *1 mark*

The testator should write a letter of wishes indicating that the spouse is to benefit.   *1 mark*

The letter of wishes is not binding on the trustees but would usually be followed unless circumstances dictate otherwise.   *1 mark*
Total: 4 marks

(b)   Under s 3 Trustee Act 2000, the trustees are given power of investment.   *1 mark*

The trustees can make any kind of investment they could make if they were absolutely entitled to the assets of the trust.   *1 mark*

This is known as the 'general power of investment'.   *1 mark*

The general power of investment applies to all trusts whenever created.   *1 mark*

However, it is subject to the settlor's wishes as set out in the trust instrument.   *1 mark*

The general power of investment does not apply to investments in land.   *1 mark*

However, under s 8 Trustee Act 2000, the trustees have powers in relation to land.   *1 mark*

The trustees may acquire freehold or leasehold land in the UK as an investment or as a residence for a beneficiary or any other reason.   *1 mark*

The section applies to all trusts, subject to restrictions or exclusion in the trust instrument.   *1 mark*
Total: 10 marks mark

(c)   An accumulation is an instruction to the trustees to accumulate income rather than pay it out to beneficiaries.   *1 mark*

The position is now governed by the Law of Property Act (LPA) 1925, as amended by the Perpetuities and Accumulations Act 1964.   *1 mark*

In this case, accumulation can only occur within either: *1 mark*

(i)   the period of 21 years from the death of the settlor, or

(ii)   the minority of any persons living at the death of the settlor (ie the grandchildren).   *1 mark*

If the accumulation period may exceed the perpetuity period for the trust, the direction to accumulate will be void.   *1 mark*

If the direction is void, the income will pass to those who would have been entitled to it if no direction had been made.   *1 mark*

If the accumulation period exceeds the maximum accumulation period allowed by law, but not the perpetuity period, only the excess will be void.   *1 mark*
Total: 7 marks

BPP
PROFESSIONAL EDUCATION

(d) A new trustee may be appointed because a trustee has died.

1 mark

1 mark

The relevant provision is the Trustee Act 1925 section 36.

The persons who can appoint the new trustee in this case are:

1 mark (i) a person nominated in the will as having the power to appoint trustees.

1 mark (ii) if none, the surviving trustees.

1 mark

Trustees must be appointed in writing and a deed will be required if there is no other instrument vesting the property in the trustees.

Total: 5 marks

Tutor's comments

This was a difficult question involving a detailed knowledge of trusts. It was important to pay attention to the mark allocation to see how much detail was required.

A nil rate band discretionary trust is a frequently used tax planning device and you should be aware of how the trust works and its advantages. Practical implications are as important as technical details in the exam, so make sure you know the points made in part (a)(iii).

Accumulations and perpetuities are a difficult area of trust law. Remember that both are designed to stop property being tied up in trust too long.

56 BILL WATTS

2 marks (a) The life tenant is **Mary** and the remainderman is **Dick**.

1 mark

The trustees have a duty to be fair to both the life tenant and the remainderman.

2 marks

Because the patent is a wasting asset which expires in 2016, **Dick might not inherit anything/have no benefit from patent**.

2 marks

The trustees have a duty to convert (ie sell assets and reinvest).

1 mark *1 mark*

They must realise the patent for cash and re-invest within one year of the death of the testator (Bill).

2 marks

2 marks

1 mark

Total: 14 marks

The new investment would be more equitable and produce capital for Dick as well as income for Mary.

Until conversion, the trustees have a **duty to apportion** the income from the trust to give a fair return to both Mary and Dick.

1 mark (b) The trustee cannot be dismissed on Mary's request.

The trustee can only be replaced under one of the following circumstances:

1 mark • He dies

1 mark • He wishes to resign/retire

1 mark • He refuses to act

1 mark • He becomes insane/incapable of acting

1 mark • He is out of the UK for more than one year

Total: 6 marks • He is in breach of duty

2 marks (c) (i) The settlor (Mary) intends to create an A&M trust for **her own son** who is a **minor**.

2 marks

Total: 4 marks The income used for Dick's benefit will be taxed as if it were Mary's.

2 marks (ii) Capital gains made by the **trustees** are taxed at a rate of 40%.

1 mark

When trustees realise assets and distribute the cash to beneficiaries there is no further CGT to pay (no exit charge).

The trustees have an annual CGT allowance of £4,100 half individual's allowance.

1 mark
Total: 4 marks

(iii) The gift is a PET.

2 marks

If the donor lives 7 years, no IHT.

1 mark

If the donor dies within 7 years, the gift becomes retrospectively chargeable subject to tapering relief.

2 marks
Total: 5 marks

(iv) • In a discretionary trust no beneficiary has an interest in possession/forms no part of his estate.

1 mark

• There is therefore no IHT charge on his death.

1 mark

• To make up for loss of tax there is a **periodic charge every 10 years**.

1 mark

• There is also an exit charge when property leaves the trust or becomes subject to interest in possession.

2 marks

• An A&M trust is not subject to a periodic charge and there is no exit charge on becoming entitled to an interest in possession/entitled to property.

1 mark
1 mark
Total: 7 marks

57 DONALD MANTON

(a) Holiday cottage

	£	£	£	
Rental income		11,000		*1 mark*
Less: Expenses				*1 mark*
Wear and tear allowance (10% × 11,000)	1,100			*1 mark*
Ground rent	75			*1 mark*
Letting agency	1,100			*1 mark*
Accountancy	500	(2,775)		
Assessable rental income			8,225	

Lease on rental shop

		£	£	
				1 mark
Premium		17,000		*2 marks*
Less: (20-1) × £17,000 × 20%		(6,460)		*1 mark*
		10,540		*1 mark*
Add: rent		2,000		*1 mark*
Assessable			12,540	

Main residence – rent-a-room

	£	£	
			1 mark
Yearly rental	6,200		*1 mark*
Less: rent-a-room relief	(4,250)		*1 mark*
Assessable		1,950	*1 mark*

Total: 15 marks

No expenses allowable if rent-a-room relief claimed.

(b)

	£	£	
Pension		22,600	
Gilts		5,000	
			1 mark
Series 18 Pensioner Bonds			*1 mark*
£15,000 × 4.75%		712	*1 mark*
Ordinary account			
£20,000 × 1.35%	270		*1 mark*
Less: tax free 1st	(70)		*1 mark*
		200	*1 mark*
Gross taxable income		28,512	

1 mark ISA – tax free

1 mark Savings certificates – tax free

Total: 8 marks (c) (i) Post 5.4.98 holding

1 mark

	£
Proceeds $\frac{2,400}{12,400} \times £31,000$	6,000

1 mark
1 mark

Less: cost	(5,500)
Gain	500

No taper relief – not held 3 years

1 mark FA 1985 Pool

1 mark

	£
Proceeds $\frac{10,000}{12,400} \times £31,000$	25,000

1 mark
1 mark

Less: cost	(26,500)
Loss	(1,500)

1 mark No indexation allowance available to increase loss.

Total: 8 marks (ii)

	£
Sale proceeds	20,000
Less: cost	

1 mark

2 marks
1 mark

$£12,000 \times \dfrac{20}{20+15}$	(6,857)
Unindexed gain	13,143
Less: indexation allowance to April 1998	

1 mark

$0.787 \times £6,857$

1 mark
Total: 6 marks

Indexed gain	(5,396)
	7,747

(iii)

1 mark
1 mark
1 mark
2 marks

	Cost £	31.3.82 MV £
Gains		
Proceeds	150,000	150,000
Less cost	(20,000)	
31.3.82		(25,000)
Unindexed gain	130,000	125,000

1 mark

2 marks

1 mark
Total: 9 marks

Less: indexation allowance		
$1.047 \times £25,000$	(26,175)	(26,175)
Indexed gain	103,825	98,825
Lower gain applies		98,825

(iv)

	£	£	
Non business assets			
Gain on unit trust units	500		*1 mark*
Less: loss (part)	(500)	Nil	*1 mark*
			1 mark
Land gain	7,747		*1 mark*
Less: loss (remainder)	(1,000)		
Net gain	6,747		
Ownership period – 6.4.98 – 5.4.04 =			*1 mark*
6 years plus additional year = 7 years			
75% × 6,747		5,060	*1 mark*
Business asset			
Shares	98,825		
Ownership period – 6.4.98 – 5.4.04 =		24,706	*1 mark*
6 years 25% × 98,825			
Chargeable gains		29,766	*1 mark*
Less: AE		(8,200)	*1 mark*
Taxable gains		21,566	

Total: 9 marks

(d)

	Non-savings £	Savings £	Total £	
Sch A				
- holiday cottage	8,225			
- shop	12,540			
- residence	1,950			*1 mark*
	22,715			
Pension	22,600			
Gilts		5,000		
Pensioner Bonds		712		
Ordinary a/c		200		
STI	45,315	5,912	51,227	*1 mark*
Less: PA	(4,745)		(4,745)	*1 mark*
Taxable income	40,570	5,912	46,482	

Tax	£	
£2,020 @ 10%	202	*1 mark*
£29,380 @ 22%	6,464	*1 mark*
£15,082 @ 40%	6,033	*1 mark*
Income tax payable	12,699	

CGT		
£21,566 @ 40%	8,626	*1 mark*

Total: 7 marks

(e) To qualify as FHL, the following conditions apply:

(i)   it must be furnished.

1 mark

(ii)   it is available for commercial letting.

1 mark

(iii)   it is available for at least 140 days per tax year.

1 mark

(iv)   it is actually let for at least 70 days in that period.

1 mark

(v)   for at least 7 months (including the 70 days) it is not normally let to the same tenant for more than 31 days.

2 marks

Total: 6 marks

(f) Rollover relief conditions:

1 mark   (i)   old asset (cottage) used in business (includes FHL)

1 mark   (ii)   private use proportion not available for relief

1 mark   (iii)   new asset acquired to be used in business (includes FHL)

1 mark   (iv)   whole proceeds need to be reinvested to defer whole gain

1 mark
1 mark   (v)   partial relief if not whole proceeds invested

Total: 6 marks   (vi)   time for investment – one year before to three years after disposal of cottage

Tutor's comments

Be careful in this question to answer the questions set exactly and to tackle the question logically.

On the rental premium calculation, make sure you charge the income element not the capital element.

Watch out for the first £70 of interest in the National Savings Ordinary account being exempt.

Look again at the loss relief and interaction with taper relief if you were not familiar with this point.

On the 'conditions' questions, usually one point will be awarded for each rule, so bear this in mind when planning your answer.

58   TOM JONES

(a) (i)   Earned income

		£
1 mark	Salary 7/12 × £42,000	24,500
1 mark	Pension 5/12 × £16,000	6,667
1 mark	Investment income	6,000
1 mark	Exercise of share option - 4,000 × (4.10 – 2.6)	6,000
1 mark	Severance pay £60,000 – £30,000 tax free	30,000
1 mark	STI	73,167
1 mark	Less personal allowance	(4,745)
1 mark	Taxable income	68,422
1 mark	Lump sum is not taxable as income	
1 mark		
1 mark	2,020 @ 10%	202
1 mark	29,380 @ 22%	6,464
1 mark	37,022 @ 40%	14,809
	Tax Liability	21,475

Total: 14 marks

(ii) **National Insurance**

Salary only, not pension or severance

Primary contributions monthly threshold £395

	£
Upper monthly limit £2,643	
(2,643 – 395) @ 11% × 7 months =	£1,730.96
(3,500 – 2,643) @ 1% × 7 months =	59.99
Total	1,790.95

1 mark

1 mark
1 mark
1 mark

Total: 4 marks

(b) A bare trust has the disadvantage that the grandchildren will become entitled to the trust assets at the age of 18. Tom has stated that he wishes to defer this until the age of 21.

1 mark
1 mark

Also a bare trust arrangement will not allow the flexibility to include as yet unborn children.

1 mark
Total: 3 marks

(c) (i) The transfer of £60,000 into the A & M trust is a Potentially Exempt Transfer (PET).

1 mark

It will not be subject to tax unless Tom dies within 7 years of the gift.

1 mark

He has made no earlier gifts and thus the gift would be within the Nil Rate Band.

1 mark

Thus under current legislation there will be no death tax to pay. Although £60,000 of the nil rate band available on death would be used up by the PET if Tom died within 7 years of the transfer to the trust.

1 mark

However the £60,000 could become chargeable until the end of the 7 year period.

1 mark

His estate is greater than £263,000 and thus would be subject to additional IHT at 40%.

1 mark
Total: 6 marks

(ii) Thus the most appropriate policy will be a 7 year intervivos term assurance to cover the additional liability on the death estate.

1 mark

Sum assured to be £60,000 × 40% = £24,000.

1 mark

Tom will be the life assured and the grantee of the policy.

2 marks
Total: 4 marks

(iii) It should be written under a flexible (power of appointment) trust, to provide for future flexibility.

1 mark

Tom can be one of the trustees to retain some control over the ultimate beneficiaries.

1 mark

He should not be the sole trustee - as flexibility might be needed immediately after his death.

1 mark

Thus add his daughters (plus possibly the family solicitor).

1 mark

The beneficiaries should ultimately be the same as under his main will. This is since it is they who will potentially be liable for the IHT. The class(es) of beneficiaries should give the trustees scope to achieve this.

1 mark
1 mark
1 mark

His daughters should be the default beneficiaries.

Total: 8 marks

(d) (i) The beneficiaries need not be named individually, they can be described as a class - 'my grandchildren'.

1 mark
1 mark

One or more of the grandchildren must acquire at least a life interest in the capital by age 25 at the latest.

The beneficiary does not have to receive the capital.

1 mark
1 mark

It is possible for the income to be for the grandchild and the capital to pass to another person.

1 mark
Total: 5 marks

BPP PROFESSIONAL EDUCATION

Until that age the trustees can accumulate the income or use it for the purpose of education or maintenance of the children.

2 marks

(ii) The trustees will be liable for a total of 40% tax on income, except dividend income, where the rate is 32.5%.

1 mark

If the income is distributed to the beneficiaries they will receive it with a 40% tax credit.

1 mark

They may be able to recover all or part of the tax depending on their personal tax circumstances.

1 mark

The trustees are also chargeable to CGT.

1 mark

They have an annual exemption which is currently ½ of the individual allowance of £8,200 ie £4,100.

1 mark

The rate of CGT is 40%.

1 mark

Cash is being transferred into the trust thus there is no 'disposal' and no charge to CGT at this point.

1 mark

Transfers of capital out of the trust to the beneficiaries are however likely to be chargeable.

Total: 9 marks

(iii) There are no periodic IHT charges for A & M trusts (as compared with other forms of discretionary trusts).

1 mark

1 mark

There is no IHT charge as such when an individual becomes entitled to income.

1 mark

However from that point in time the relevant proportion of the underlying assets are deemed to be in their estate for their own IHT purposes.

Total: 3 marks

(e) (i) It would be advisable for Tom himself to be one of the trustees to retain some control.

1 mark

1 mark

It is possible for beneficiaries to be trustees.

1 mark

But minors cannot be expressly appointed as trustees – thus effectively excluding the existing grandchildren.

1 mark
1 mark
1 mark
Total: 6 marks

Their parents (Tom's children) would however be suitable trustees as they would have an interest in the successful management of the investments. In addition they might like to appoint the family solicitor/accountant as a professional adviser.

1 mark

(ii) The trust will vest in the remaining trustee(s).

1 mark

The trust deed should give specific powers of appointment.

2 marks

Otherwise the surviving trustees or the personal representative of the last dead trustee can appoint new trustees.

Total: 4 marks

1 mark
1 mark
1 mark
Total: 3 marks

(iii) The general principle is that trustees should not profit from their position. They will not be able to charge. Unless the terms of the trust expressly make provision for their remuneration.

1 mark

(f) (i) ISA – not available to under 18s (except cash ISAs for 16 to 17 year olds).

1 mark

Cannot be held in trust.

Total: 2 marks
1 mark

(ii) High yielding corporate bond – income will attract 40% tax and it is not planned to distribute it – thus less attractive.

1 mark
Total: 2 marks

Also capital is potentially at risk of erosion in real terms.

(iii) Index linked gilts offer a good prospect of real return, little tax as low level of income return.

1 mark
1 mark

Tutor's comments

Total: 2 marks

There were some more difficult items in the income tax computation in part (a) (eg the share option and severance pay), but enough basic items to gain a pass mark.

The difficult conditions for types of trust must be known. Note the practical implications too.

A basic description of IT/CGT on trusts has been a common topic. Remember that discretionary trusts pay IT and CGT at 40% (32.5% for dividends) with effect from 6 April 2004.

The power of appointing trustees under s36 Trustee Act 1925 are often examined and are the most important method of appointing trustees.

59 DAVID STAMP

(a) (i)

	£	
Goodwill		
All gain	100,000	*1 mark*
Shop		
Proceeds	150,000	
Less: cost	(30,000)	*1 mark*
enhancement	(25,000)	*1 mark*
	95,000	*1 mark*
Less: indexation allowance 0.703 × £30,000	(21,090)	
Indexed gain	73,910	
Total gains	173,910	*1 mark*
Ownership period 6.4.98 – 5.4.04 = 6 years (even for enhancement)		*1 mark*
25% × 173,910	43,477	*1 mark*
Less: annual exemption	(8,200)	*1 mark*
Taxable gains	35,277	*1 mark*
Tax 31,400 – 27,500 = 3,900 @ 20%	780	*1 mark*
31,377 @ 40%	12,551	*1 mark*
CGT Payable	13,331	*Total: 11 marks*

(ii) **Roll over relief** may be granted on the purchase of furnished holiday accommodation.

- The gain before tapering would be deferred.
- Must reinvest whole proceeds to roll over whole gain
- Invest within three years of sale to obtain relief

1 mark
1 mark
1 mark
1 mark
1 mark

(b) (i)

Total: 4 marks

	£	
Sale Proceeds	75,000	*1 mark*
Purchase Price	(50,000)	*1 mark*
Chargeable Gain	25,000	*1 mark*
		1 mark
Divide chargeable gain by number years held (5)		*1 mark*
to calculate top slice		*1 mark*
Top slice is therefore	5,000	

1 mark	Add top slice to income in 2004/05
1 mark	31,400 – 27,500 no tax on slice
1 mark	Basic rate has been paid
Total: 12 marks	32,500 – 31,400 tax @ 18% (40% – 22%) = £198
	Total tax on slice is therefore £198
	Total tax payable would be 5 × £198 = £990 on bond

2 marks

(ii) The whole of the £40,000 partial encashment would be treated as chargeable gain after allowable withdrawals

1 mark

(iii)
- Segmentation allows encashment of individual whole bonds to effect a partial encashment as each segment is treated as an individual policy.

1 mark
1 mark
Total: 3 marks

- Chargeable gain is then sale price less purchase price for each individual segment which reduces overall gain.

(c) Net dividends grossed up:

		£	£
1 mark	£6,000 × 100/90	6,667	
	Less expenses grossed up		
1 mark	£800 × 100/90	(889)	
1 mark			5,778
1 mark	Building Society interest grossed up		
2 marks	£3,200 × 100/80	4,000	
1 mark	Tax Admin expenses 889 × 10%		89
Total: 7 marks	Remaining dividends 5,778 × 32.5%		1,878
	Other income 4,000 × 40%		1,600
			3,567

(d) (i) **Quick succession relief will apply**

2 marks

In this case the property would be subject to IHT twice in a short space of time.

1 mark
1 mark

Relief means that credit is given for a proportion of the tax paid on the first occasion.

1 mark
Total: 5 marks

Because deaths occur within one year, 100% relief is given.

1 mark

(ii) Normally there is unlimited exemption for transfers between spouses.

2 marks

An exception is made where the UK domiciled spouse gives to a foreign domiciled spouse.

1 mark

In this case exemption is **limited** to £55,000.

1 mark
Total: 5 marks

Concepta does not qualify under the deemed domicile rule has not been resident for last 17/20 years.

(iii) If David retains his UK domicile he is subject to UK IHT on all property owned by him in both **UK** and **overseas.**

2 marks
2 marks
1 mark
Total: 5 marks

- David could change his domicile to **Domicile of choice.**
- To do this he needs to **permanently reside abroad** with the **intention of never returning to live in the UK on a permanent basis.**

1 mark
1 mark
1 mark
1 mark
Total: 4 marks

(e)
- Enduring power of attorney
- Only takes effect once registered with the court of protection
- May only be registered once Albert is incapable of managing his own affairs
- Unlike an ordinary power of attorney it is not revoked upon Albert becoming incapable.

(f) Three components can be held in ISAs

    (i) Cash component – building society/bank; units in unauthorised or qualifying money market fund; National Savings products **other than** savings certificates and premium bonds   *3 marks*

    (ii) Insurance component – life policy on life of ISA investor alone. Must not be a regular premium policy. Must constitute 'long term' business   *3 marks*

    (iii) Stocks and shares components – shares or loan stock issued by company. Gilts (minimum term 5 years left). Authorised unit trust, OEIC, UCITS or DIs.   *3 marks*
    Total: 9 marks

(g) (i) David may make a gift aid declaration   *1 mark*
- David pays net amount   *1 mark*
- Charity can reclaim tax from Inland Revenue   *1 mark*
    Total: 3 marks

    (ii)
- Lump sum gift falls under gift aid   *1 mark*
- Payment made net of income tax   *1 mark*
- Basic rate tax reclaimed by charity   *1 mark*
- David can obtain relief for higher rate tax   *1 mark*
- Gift free from IHT   *1 mark*
    Total: 5 marks

60 KEITH AND ANN

(a) (i) **Income tax**
- Since this is a parental gift the income will be taxed as if it were still Keith's if the income is in excess of £100 pa per child.   *1 mark*
- Income tax would therefore be payable at 40%.   *1 mark*
    1 mark
    Total: 3 marks

    (ii) **Capital Gains Tax**
- Since the asset being transferred into the trust is cash, there can be no CGT on the transfer in.   *2 marks*
- Gains made within the trust are assessed against the children.   *1 mark*
- The annual exemption will be £8,200 per child.   *1 mark*
    Total: 4 marks

    (iii) **IHT**
- The transfer in will be a PET.   *1 mark*
- No IHT will be payable providing Keith survives for 7 years after the transfer.   *1 mark*
    1 mark
- The assets of each trust will form part of each child's estate.   *Total: 3 marks*

(b) (i)
- One or more of the beneficiaries must become entitled to, or to at least have achieved an interest in possession in the settled property, no later than their 25th birthday.   *1 mark*
- Before that time the beneficiaries do not have a right to income.   *1 mark*
- The vesting age must be specified at outset.   *1 mark*
- The trustees accumulate income if not paid or applied for the maintenance, education or benefit of a beneficiary until the vesting age is reached.   *1 mark*
- Either not more than 25 years have elapsed since the trust was set up or all the beneficiaries had a common grandparent.   *1 mark*
    Total: 6 marks

(ii)
- There would be no CGT liability on the transfer of cash into the trust.
- Gains realised by the trustees will be able to use the trustee's annual exemption of $\frac{1}{2} \times £8,200 = £4,100$.
- The rate of CGT will be 40%.
- The transfer out of the trust will also be a CGT disposal.
- Gift relief will be available on all assets.

1 mark
1 mark
1 mark
1 mark
1 mark
Total: 5 marks

(iii)
- Section 31 TA 1925 is a statutory power which enables trustees to pay out income to infant beneficiaries.
- However at the age of 18 the beneficiary will be deemed to be entitled to the income - they will have an interest in possession.
- When the capital is advanced to such a beneficiary subsequently, the CGT can be held over only in respect of business assets.
- S 31 can be excluded, expressly or impliedly, or varied.
- For example, to postpone the right to income until capital vests at 25.

1 mark
1 mark
1 mark
1 mark
1 mark
1 mark
Total: 7 marks

(c) (i)
- The bond will suffer tax on income and gains at a rate of 20/22% within the fund.
- The bond does not produce income as such.
- Keith is a parental settlor and would therefore be liable to income tax in respect of the trust.
- If the bond is managed to avoid a chargeable event.
- Withdrawals should not exceed the 5% pa allowance.
- There will be no income tax liability on Keith.
- The bond can then be assigned to the children.
- An assignment which is not for money's worth is not a chargeable event.
- If this is done when they have reached age 18.
- Subsequent chargeable events will be assessed on the children only.

2 marks
1 mark
2 marks
1 mark
1 mark
1 mark
1 mark
1 mark
1 mark
1 mark
Total: 12 marks

(ii)
- Zero coupon prefs do not pay an income.
- Thus there is no risk of the income being assessed on Keith/CGT is not payable as a result of parental settlor relationships.
- The return on Zeros is treated as capital gains - liable to CGT.
- Trustees will be liable for CGT after indexation of the cost and tapering.
- The trustees will have an annual allowance of £4,100.
- The rate of CGT, if payable, will be 40%.

1 mark
1 mark
1 mark
2 marks
1 mark
1 mark
Total: 7 marks

(d) Value of Keith's estate for intestacy purposes

Personal effects	15,000
Investments	80,000
$\frac{1}{2}$ share in house	100,000
Sum assured under the endowment policy	65,000
Total	260,000

- His wife will inherit £125,000 outright, plus his personal effects (£140,000 total) and a life interest in £60,000.
- On her death the capital base of the £60,000 life interest will pass to their children.
- The children will each receive £30,000 outright but this will be held in trust until they reach the age of 18.

1 mark
1 mark
1 mark
1 mark
2 marks
1 mark
1 mark
1 mark
1 mark
Total: 10 marks

(e) Without the survivorship clause the second death will give rise to an IHT charge of

	355,000
Less NRB	(263,000)
	92,000

1 mark

2 marks

Tax at 40% = £36,800

1 marks

Total: 4 marks

With a survivorship clause there would be no IHT since each estate is less than the NRB

(f) (i)
- Under such wills, the executors hold the property on a discretionary trust which gives them wide powers to appoint within a specified group of individuals.

2 marks

- A power of appointment enables a person other than the testator to determine who gets what.

2 marks

- The surviving spouse is normally a trustee and is a potential beneficiary.

2 marks

- To be effective the power of appointment should be made within the period of three months and two years of the death.

2 marks

- IHT is charged as if the gifts or trusts had been made at the time of death, eg to use spouse exemption.

2 marks

Total: 10 marks

(ii)
- It enables the nil rate band of the first to die spouse to be used.

1 mark

- Flexibility is provided so that the estate can be allocated to suit the prevailing tax and personal situations at the time of death.

2 marks

- The surviving spouse still has access to the estate if required.

1 mark

Total: 4 marks

61 JOE POLLARD

(a) (i) The first lump sum payment is exempt from IHT, under the spouse exemption.

2 marks

This applies up to decree absolute.

1 mark

It does not apply after that date.

1 mark

Total: 4 marks

(ii) The second lump sum payment is a disposition, because Joe's estate decreases.

However, it is not a transfer of value because there was no gratuitous intent.

1 mark

Therefore it will not have immediate inheritance consequences.

1 mark

(iii) The transfer of the cottage was a potentially exempt transfer (PET).

1 mark

Total: 3 marks

However, it is now exempt because Joe has survived seven years from the date of the gift.

1 mark

The current value of the cottage is still in Joe's estate, however.

1 mark

This is because it is a gift with reservation of benefit as Joe has free use of the cottage for a substantial period each year.

1 mark

Total: 4 marks

(iv) The value of the dental practice could qualify for business property relief as it is an unincorporated business.

1 mark

However, if Joe died in April 2004, no relief would be given.

1 mark

This is because Joe has not owned the business for two years.

1 mark

If Joe did die in June 2004, business property relief would be available as the two year ownership period has been satisfied.

2 marks

The rate of relief would be 100%.

1 mark

Total: 6 marks

(b)　(i)　Estate – date of death 12 April 2004

	£	£
Dental practice	375,000	
Less: loan secured	(200,000)	
Net value of practice		175,000
House		170,000
Cottage in Cornwall		45,000
Quoted shares		
150,000 × 50.25p	75,375	
Add: dividends		
150,000 × 0.08	12,000	
Total value of shares		87,375
Building society a/c		20,000
Pension scheme		85,000
Gross estate		582,375
Less: liabilities		
Income tax	45,000	
Unsecured loan (mother)	25,000	
		(70,000)
Net estate for IHT		512,375

1 mark (×15)
Total: 15 marks

(ii)　IHT payable

No lifetime transfers within 7 years of death

	£
Net estate as above	512,375
Less: nil rate band	(263,000)
Estate chargeable @ 40%	249,375
Tax payable	99,750

1 mark (×4)
Total: 5 marks

(c)　(i)　Joe has not yet nominated a beneficiary of his personal pension scheme.

He should at least nominate Laura to receive the fund.

To achieve more flexibility he could place the benefit in trust.

Neither action would constitute a chargeable transfer for IHT.

The tax saving would be £85,000 × 40% = £34,000.

1 mark (several)
Total: 5 marks

(ii)　The cottage is currently in Joe's estate as a gift with reservation of benefit.

Joe should either stop using the cottage or pay a market rent for his use.

The cessation of the reservation would be a PET.

Joe would have to survive seven years from the cessation for IHT to cease to be chargeable on the PET.

If he survived 7 years, the tax saved would be £45,000 × 40% = £18,000.

2 marks / 1 mark
Total: 6 marks

(d)　(i)　The trust is a discretionary trust.

The trust must account for further tax on income available for distribution, ie after income expenses.

The rate of tax on dividend income is 32.5% ie a further 22.5% payable by the trustees.

Total: 4 marks

The rate of tax on other income is 40% ie a further 20% payable by the trustees.

(ii)

	Savings income £	Dividend income £	
Dividends			
£15,750 × 100/90		17,500	*1 mark*
BSI			*1 mark*
£3,600 × 100/80	4,500		*1 mark*
Taxable income	4,500	17,500	
Less: expenses			
£450 × 100/90			*1 mark*
(set off v divis 1st)		(500)	*1 mark*
Income at rate applicable to trusts	4,500	17,000	*1 mark*

Tax

	£	£	
On £500 @ 10%		50	*1 mark*
On £17,000 @ 32.5%		5,525	*1 mark*
On £4,500 @ 40%		1,800	*1 mark*
Total tax liability		7,375	*1 mark*
Less: Tax suffered			
£17,500 @ 10%	1,750		*1 mark*
£4,500 @ 20%	900		*1 mark*
			Total:12 marks
		(2,650)	
Tax to pay		4,725	

(e) A transfer to a charitable trust is an exempt transfer for IHT.   *1 mark*

A transfer to a non-charitable trust may be subject to IHT.   *1 mark*

Income of a charitable trust is free of income tax.   *1 mark*

Income of a non-charitable trust is taxable to income tax.   *1 mark*
1 mark

Capital gains made by a charitable trust is generally exempt from CGT.   *1 mark*
Total: 6 marks

Capital gains of a non-charitable trust is usually chargeable.

(f) Joe could acquire the shares by investing in an individual savings account (ISA).   *1 mark*

He could invest up to £7,000 in a maxi-ISA in 2004/05.   *1 mark*

He could invest a further £7,000 in a maxi-ISA in future years.   *1 mark*

Income in the ISA is free of income tax.   *1 mark*

Capital gains on shares in an ISA are free of capital gains tax.   *1 mark*
Total: 5 marks

Tutor's comments

BPR on the dental surgery business was a slightly tricky point, although the examiner did identify the crucial dates. If you did not know what the question was asking, look back at your study text!

The income tax implications of a discretionary trust should be studied carefully. Note the different treatment of dividends and other income.

Where differences between trusts are asked for in a question, make sure you highlight these rather than listing the tax on each type of trust.

Mock exam 1

ADVANCED FINANCIAL PLANNING CERTIFICATE
G10-TAXATION AND TRUSTS

SPECIAL NOTICES

- All questions in this paper are based on English law and practice applicable in the 2004/05 tax year, unless stated otherwise, and should be answered accordingly.

- Assume all individuals are domiciled, resident and ordinarily resident in the UK unless stated otherwise.

INSTRUCTIONS

- **Three hours are allowed for this paper.**

- **READ THE INSTRUCTIONS OVERLEAF CAREFULLY BEFORE ANSWERING ANY QUESTIONS.**

- If you wish to use a calculator in this examination, it must be a silent battery or solar powered calculator.

G10: Taxation and trusts

CANDIDATE INSTRUCTIONS

READ THE INSTRUCTRIONS BELOW BEFORE ANSWERING ANY QUESTIONS.

Three hours are allowed for this paper. You should answer all questions in Sections A and B, and two out of three questions in Section C.

The paper carries a total of 200 marks, as follows:

> Section A: 45 marks
> Section B: 75 marks
> Section C: 80 marks

You are advised to spend approximately 40 minutes on Section A, and 70 minutes each on Sections B and C. You are strongly advised to attempt ALL the required questions in order to gain maximum possible marks.

The number of marks allocated to each question part is given next to the question and you should spend your time in accordance with that allocation.

Tax tables are provided at the front of this kit.

Answer each question on a new page and leave several lines blank after each question part.

It is important to show all steps in a calculation, even if you have used a calculator.

Please ensure that you understand the Special Notices printed in the box on the previous page.

> *Subject to providing sufficient detail, you are advised to be as brief and concise as possible, using note format and short sentences on separate lines wherever possible.*

SECTION A

Answer all questions in this section, which carries 45 marks.

1   (a)   What are the two standard investment criteria under the Trustee Act 2000?   (2)

    (b)   What must the trustees generally do before exercising any power of investment?   (2)

    (c)   In what circumstances do the trustees **not** have to follow the procedure you outlined in (b) above. Give an example.   (3)

    (d)   What further duties do the trustees have in relation to investments they have made?   (2)

2   Owen is a self employed landscape gardener. He was sent a tax return for 2003/04 in May 2004. It is now 10 August 2005 and he has just filed his return and paid the balancing payment due of £5,000.

    Explain the penalties, interest and surcharges the Inland Revenue could charge Owen for 2003/04.   (5)

3   Paula Wilson founded a fashion company a few years ago. Paula Wilson owns 45% of the shares. The other major shareholder, Ellen Brook, owns 35% of the shares with the remaining 20% owned by Ellen's husband, Derek.

    The value of the shareholdings is as follows:

%	£
20	18,000
35	31,500
45	40,500
55	60,000

    Derek gives his shares to his son, Peter. Explain how the transfer will be valued for inheritance tax purposes and calculate the value of the transfer.   (7)

4   Explain the capital gains tax treatment of the following investments:

    (i)   Shares in an unquoted trading company acquired 2001   (1)
    (ii)   10% Treasury Stock 2008   (1)
    (iii) Shares in ICI plc held in an ISA   (1)
    (iv)   Vase worth £5,000 acquired two years ago for £3,000   (1)

5   Sam bought Wildmarsh, a 40 acre agricultural pasture, for £100,000 in April 1982.

    In September 2004 Sam sold 10 acres of Wildmarsh to BSE Industries plc for £20,000. Sam is advised by his surveyor that the remaining 30 acres have a value of £30,000.

    Calculate, **showing your workings**, the capital loss arising on the disposal in September 2004.   (5)

6   Ivor Novel set up a trust five and a half years ago with his daughter as the life tenant and his only grandchild as the remainderman. Ivor put £350,000 into the trust.

Ivor's daughter was killed in an accident two months ago. At the time of her death the trust property was valued at £380,000.

What is the inheritance tax position:

(a) for Ivor?   (3)
(b) on the death of the life tenant?   (5)

7   Molly is aged 62. Her income is £31,000 p.a. She invested £100,000 into a single premium investment bond of Everlasting Life plc, a UK insurance company, on 12 February 1999. The bond consisted of 20 identical policies. She has made no previous withdrawals from the bond.

Owing to a family crisis, Molly will have to take £50,000 from the bond on 3 March 2005. This can be done by encashing eight policies or simply by a withdrawal of £50,000 across all policies.

Calculate **showing all workings** the top slice of the gain arising, assuming the £50,000 is raised by:

(a) encashing eight policies   (4)
(b) withdrawing £50,000 across all policies equally   (3)

SECTION B

This question is compulsory and carries 75 marks.

8   Michael and Julia were married 3 years ago. It was a second marriage for both of them. Michael had previously been married to Sandra, who died in 1996. Michael and Sandra had two children, Rory and Elizabeth, both of whom are now grown up and married with young children. Julia had no children from her first marriage, which ended in divorce many years ago. Michael is now aged 70 and Julia is 62.

Michael retired when he was 65. He receives a pension from his former employer of £12,500 (PAYE deducted £1,178) and a state retirement pension of £6,280. He also received net interest from the Eastern Rock Building Society of £504.

Michael inherited a fairly substantial amount of capital from Sandra and on 10 August 2004 he set up a power of appointment trust with £150,000. The wide class of potential beneficiaries include Rory and Elizabeth and their children. The default beneficiaries are Rory and Elizabeth in equal shares. This was the first inheritance tax transfer made by Michael. The trust is invested in fixed interest unit trust units and in single premium linked investment bonds.

Michael had taken out a with-profits bond on 1 March 2000 investing £20,000. He made withdrawals of 5% on each anniversary of the investment. Michael surrendered the bond on 15 January 2005 and received £21,000.

The current value of Michael and Julia's assets are as follows:

	Michael £	Julia £
House		200,000
Eastern Rock Building Society	15,000	
National Savings	60,000	34,000
PEP accounts	200,000	
ISA accounts	40,000	15,000
Totals	315,000	249,000

There are no jointly held assets.

Michael's current will leaves his estate to his children, with substitutional gifts to his grandchildren if his children should predecease him. He is concerned that Julia will not have sufficient ready money to live on after his death, but is concerned that the capital will not pass outright to Julia as he wishes it to be available to benefit his children and grandchildren. Julia has made a will leaving the house to Michael and the rest of her estate to various UK charities.

Questions

(a) Calculate, **showing all your workings**, the amount of any tax payable or repayable to Michael for 2004/05.   **(26)**

(b) The Eastern Rock Building Society has voted to de-mutualise. Michael can choose to receive cash or shares on the de-mutualisation. Explain the CGT implications if Michael chooses to receive:

   (i)   cash   **(7)**

   (ii)   shares   **(3)**

(c) Describe the inheritance tax treatment of the transfer into the flexible power of appointment trust. **(6)**

(d) Explain the inheritance tax implications of the flexible power of appointment trust in relation to the beneficiaries. **(4)**

(e) Explain the income tax treatment of the investments in the trust. **(11)**

(f) Michael has been advised to rewrite his will to include a nil rate band trust. Explain how this would operate and how it would help with his concerns about Julia and his children. **(12)**

(g) Outline why it would be preferable to re-write Michael's will to incorporate the nil rate band trust instead of relying on a post death deed of variation. **(6)**

Total marks available for Question 8: 75

SECTION C

Answer any TWO of the three questions in this section.

Each question carries 40 marks.

9 You have been approached by Jennifer Conway for financial advice. She is aged 33 and single. She is a basic rate tax payer. Jennifer was born and has lived all her life in the UK. She holds a full UK passport.

Jennifer works in hospital administration in a local, private hospital. She has, however, accepted a new contract of employment to work abroad for the next four years as a Hospital Administration Manager.

She has contributed £150 per month to an ISA since 6 April 1999 and its present value is £10,200. She would like to continue to contribute to this as long as she is able.

Both her parents are dead. Her father was the last to die seven years ago and left her his holiday house in Spain (currently valued at £75,000) and money with a current value of £158,800. This is currently deposited in a UK bank account and earns 5% gross per annum. She intends to invest £100,000 either in a distributor or non distributor fund before she goes abroad.

She owns her own property with an interest only mortgage of £35,000 covered by a low cost endowment for the same amount. The interest rate is 8%. The term remaining on the mortgage is 18 years. She is thinking about letting her home whilst she is abroad. She expects to obtain a rental income of £4,500 per annum, (after the deduction of associated management expenses). The property is currently valued at £70,000.

(a) (i) What effect if any, does her decision to work abroad have on Jennifer's domicile status? (1)

(ii) List the main tests used to determine Jennifer's residency. (4)

(b) (i) Explain the rules relating to letting income if Jennifer goes abroad. (5)

(ii) Calculate the net annual taxable income she will receive from letting her property if she decides to do this. (4)

(c) Jennifer has heard that she will not be liable for capital gains tax on the sale of her home in the UK as long as her house has been her principal residence. She believes that relief may also be available for certain periods when she is not actually living in the house and has asked you to clarify this point for her. Explain which periods are deemed to be periods of occupation for the purposes of calculating principal private residence relief. (5)

(d) (i) State Jennifer's tax position if she invests in a distributor fund. (3)

(ii) State Jennifer's tax position if she invests in a non-distributor fund. (4)

(iii) Which type of offshore fund would be most suitable for Jennifer and why? (4)

(e) (i) State the inheritance tax position for Jennifer regarding her Spanish property. (2)

(ii) Calculate any liability to inheritance tax if she had died on 1 March 2005 assuming that she has remained resident and ordinarily resident in the UK until her death. (8)

Total marks available for Question 9: 40

BPP
PROFESSIONAL EDUCATION

10   Christina Marshall aged 36 is employed as a sales manager in her husband Scott's printing company. Christina and Scott have an 18 month old son who is currently looked after by Christina's mother. Scott is a higher rate taxpayer who earns £50,000 pa.

In the tax year 2004/05 Christina will be paid a salary of £24,210 per annum and the company will pay £4,000 per annum into a personal pension for her. She is contracted into the State Second Pension Scheme. She is provided with an 1,800cc petrol driven company car (CO_2 emissions figure 195 g/km) and the company also pays all the petrol bills. The list price of the car when new in January 2002 was £14,100.

Christina owns the following investments:

£20,000 in a Jersey-based building society account with annual interest of £1,600.
£70,000 in equity unit trusts with annual dividends reinvested of £2,475.
£11,181 in a National Savings Income Bond with an interest rate of 5.59% per annum.

Christina and Scott employ Bill on a salary of £8,250. He is a widower who looks after his son aged 10. Bill works 20 hours per week to allow him to spend extra time with his son who is disabled. He also spends £140 per week on childcare costs.

Questions

(a) (i)   State how the rules governing the calculation of the value of benefits differ between employees earning less than £8,500 and directors or employees earning £8,500 or over.   **(3)**

     (ii)   Explain how the value of cheap loans are calculated for an employee earning £8,500 or over.   **(4)**

(b) (i)   Calculate the amount of income tax payable on Christina's income from all sources for the year 2004/05. **Show all your workings.**   **(22)**

     (ii)   Calculate the amount of National Insurance Christina will pay in the tax year. **Show all your workings.**   **(3)**

(c) Calculate the total tax credits which Bill will be entitled to in 2004/2005.   **(8)**

Total marks available for Question 10: 40

11   Geoffrey Evans is a 68 year old bachelor, resident and domiciled in UK. As a self-employed agricultural consultant he has a year end of 30 April and his tax adjusted earnings for the year of assessment 2004/05 were £3,750. During the tax year 2004/05 he received £7,875 net in dividend income from his portfolio and £6,800 in rent from a residential property.

Geoffrey sold two assets on 5 October 2004. The first was his total holding in C & F Investment Trust for £11,000. He bought the shares in April 1979 for £6,100 and they were valued on 31 March 1982 at £6,500. He has not made a capital gains tax rebasing election. The indexed rise between March 1982 and April 1998 was 1.047.

The second asset sold was the residential property which he acquired in May 1983 for £15,600. He spent a further £10,400 on improving the property in June 1996 and eventually sold it for £87,500. The indexed rise between May 1983 and April 1998 is 0.922 and between June 1996 and April 1998 is 0.063. Neither asset qualifies as a business asset.

He made no other disposals in the 2004/05 tax year. He has deferred taking the State Retirement Pension.

(a) Calculate, **showing all workings,** the amount of income tax Geoffrey will have to pay for the year 2004/05.   (14)

(b) Calculate, **showing all workings,** the amount of capital gains tax Geoffrey will have to pay for the tax year 2004/05.   (26)

Total marks available for Question 11: 40

Advanced Financial Planning Certificate

G10

Answers
to
Mock Exam 1

Overview of Mock Examination 1

Section A

There were two law questions and five tax questions in this section.

Trustee investment is a topical area that you should review before the actual exam.

Don't neglect the topic of how tax is paid and the consequences of not paying tax on time.

Question 7 was about a single premium bond - this topic nearly always appears in this section so make sure you are prepared for it.

Section B

This was a general tax question with lots of frequently examined points.

Good marks should have been obtained on part (a). Note the age allowance point on single premium bond profit.

Parts (c) and (d) dealt with basic IHT concepts – make sure you know these aspects.

Parts (f) and (g) dealt with estate planning. You may have had to think hard about part (g) – sometimes it's not sufficient just to know the technical content, you also have to be able to apply it in a practical situation.

Section C

Two out of three questions had to be answered.

Question 9 dealt with foreign aspects of tax and investments. There were some tricky points of detail here and you should highlight in the solution any points you missed.

Question 10 was about income tax and NICs. The main area to score marks was the income tax computation (make sure you know the layout required!). It should also have been easy to pick up the marks on the NICs with a bit of care on the figures. Part (a) required a general and detailed discussion of benefits in kind. Part (iii) required a detailed knowledge of the rules on childcare facilities - maybe too detailed knowledge to expect most students to have. The planning points in part (c) were not difficult, but you may not have thought about them before. Make sure you understand them.

Question 11 should have been the easiest question to obtain good marks on in this section. Once again, ensure that you can set up the income tax computation layout quickly. The capital gains tax computations also required standard layouts. Make sure you remember to consider both cost and 31 March 1982 values where appropriate.

ANSWERS TO MOCK EXAM 1

SECTION A

1   (a)   The standard investment criteria are:

        (i)   the suitability of investments for the trust, and   *1 mark*

        (ii)   the need for diversification of investments of the trust, to the extent that this is appropriate in the circumstances.   *1 mark*

        Total: 2 marks

  (b)   Before exercising any power of investment, the trustees must generally:

        (i)   obtain, and   *1 mark*

        (ii)   consider proper advice.   *1 mark*

      about the way that the power should be exercised.   *Total: 2 marks*

  (c)   A trustee does not have to obtain advice if he reasonably concludes that, in all the circumstances, it is:

        (i)   unnecessary, or   *1 mark*

        (ii)   inappropriate to do so.   *1 mark*

      Examples: *1 mark*

        (i)   a small investment where the cost of obtaining advice is disproportionate.   *Total: 3 marks*

        (ii)   the trustees themselves possess skills and knowledge so that separate advice is not needed.

  (d)   Trustees must from time to time, review the investments of the trust.   *1 mark*

      Having regard to the standard investment criteria, the trustees must consider whether the investments should be varied.   *1 mark*

      Total: 2 marks

2   Owen is liable to a penalty of £200.   *1 mark*

    This is because his return was delivered more than 6 months but not more than 12 months later than the due date of 31 January 2005.   *1 mark*

    Interest will be due on the late paid tax from the due date of 31 January to the day before the actual payment (191 days).   *1 mark*

    He is liable to a surcharge of 10% of the income tax paid late.   *1 mark*

    This is because the payment was more than six months after the due date of 31 January 2005.   *Total: 5 marks*

1 mark

3 The transfer of value is the difference between the value of Derek's estate before the transfer and his estate after the transfer.

1 mark
1 mark

The shareholding held by Derek will be valued as part of a larger holding, if this produces a higher value than his isolated holding.

1 mark

That larger holding is the aggregate of the holdings of Derek and his spouse Ellen under the related property rules.

1 mark

The transfer of value is therefore:

	£
Before 20/55 × 60,000	21,818
After	(nil)
Transfer of value	21,818

1 mark

1 mark

Total: 7 marks

As this is larger that his isolated holding (£18,000), the related property valuation applies.

1 mark

4 (i) chargeable asset, business taper relief applies on disposal

1 mark

(ii) exempt asset so no chargeable gain or allowable loss on disposal

1 mark

(iii) exempt asset because held in ISA

1 mark

(iv) exempt chattel worth less than £6,000

Total: 4 marks

5

	£
Proceeds	20,000

1 mark

2 mark

$$\text{Less: cost } \frac{20,000}{20,000 + 30,000} \times £100,000 \qquad (40,000)$$

1 mark

Loss (20,000)

1 mark

Indexation allowance cannot increase loss.

Total: 5 marks

1 mark
1 mark

6 (a) The original transfer to the life interest trust was a potentially exempt transfer.

1 mark

No lifetime tax was payable.

Death tax will be chargeable if Ivor dies within seven years of the transfer, which will be payable by the trustees.

Total: 3 marks

1 mark

(b) The death of the life tenant is a chargeable transfer.

2 mark

The value of the trust will be aggregated with the life tenant's free estate to work out the inheritance tax.

1 mark

The tax will then be apportioned between the trust and the free estate.

1 mark

The trust tax will be payable by the trustees out of the trust fund.

Total: 5 marks

7   (a) Surrender of eight policies

		£	
Surrender value		50,000	*1 mark*
Less: cost 8/20 × £100,000		(40,000)	*1 mark*
Profit		10,000	*1 mark*

Number of complete years since policy taken out is 6

Top slice is £10,000/6   1,667   *1 mark*

Total: 4 marks

(b) Partial surrender

		£	
Proceeds		50,000	
Less: cumulative allowance			
5% × 7 × £100,000		(35,000)	*1 mark*
Chargeable amount		15,000	*1 mark*

Number of complete years since policy taken out is 7 since event is treated as at the end of the year ie. 11 February 2006.

Top slice is £15,000/7   2,143   *1 mark*

Total: 3 marks

SECTION B

8   (a)

		Non-Savings income £	Savings income £	Total income £
1 mark	Pension	12,500		
1 mark	State retirement pension	6,280		
1 mark	BSI £504 × $^{100}/_{80}$		630	
	STI	18,780	630	19,410
1 mark	Less: PA (W)	(4,745)		(4,745)
	Taxable income	14,035	630	14,665

Tax

		£
1 mark	£2,020 × 10%	202
1 mark	£12,015 × 22%	2,643
1 mark	£630 × 20%	126
		2,971
1 mark	Less: MCAA (W)	(506)
1 mark	Tax liability	2,465
1 mark	Less: PAYE	(1,178)
1 mark	tax on BSI	(126)
1 mark	Tax to pay	1,161

Working

		£	Income £
1 mark	STI as above		19,410
	Bond profit		
1 mark	Proceeds	21,000	
1 mark	Add: withdrawals 5% × 20,000 × 4	4,000	
		25,000	
1 mark	Less: cost	(20,000)	
1 mark	Chargeable		5,000
			24,410

1 mark	*Note:* No top slicing in calculating age allowances.
1 mark	Excess income £(24,410 – 18,900) = £5,510
1 mark	Reduction ½ £2,755
	Set against PA to reduce to ordinary allowance.
1 mark	£(6,830 – 4,745) = £2,085
1 mark	Remainder £670
	Set against MCAA
1 mark	£(5,725 – 670) = £5,055
1 mark	Allowance @ 10% = £506
2 marks	*Note:* No further tax is payable on the bond as Michael is a basic rate taxpayer.

Total: 26 marks

(b) (i) If Michael has membership rights, the receipt of the cash bonus is a disposal for CGT. *1 mark*

The asset being disposed of is the membership rights attaching to the account. *1 mark*

The acquisition cost of the asset is the closing balance of the account. *1 mark*

The proceeds is the amount of the cash bonus. *1 mark*

Indexation allowance up to April 1998 will be available if appropriate. *1 mark*

Taper relief may also be available. *1 mark*

If Michael does not have membership rights, no capital gains tax will be payable on the receipt of the cash bonus. *1 mark*

Total: 7 marks

(ii) Where free shares are issued there is no CGT disposal. *1 mark*

However, the base cost of the shares will be nil. *1 mark*

Therefore, there will be a gain when the shares are disposed of. *1 mark*

Total: 3 marks

(c) £6,000 of the transfer will be covered by Michael's annual exemptions for this year and last year. *1 mark*

The remaining £144,000 transferred to the trust is a potentially exempt transfer. *1 mark*

No lifetime IHT will be payable. *1 mark*

If Michael dies within 7 years of the transfer, the PET will become chargeable. *1 mark*

No IHT will be payable by trustees as the PET is within the nil band. *1 mark*

However, £144,000 of the nil band will not be available to set against later transfers. *1 mark*

Total: 6 marks

(d) Rory and Elizabeth each have an interest in possession in half of the trust fund. *1 mark*

Half of the capital of the fund would be included in each of their estates for IHT. *1 mark*

If an appointment is made to a potential beneficiary other than Rory and Elizabeth, there would be a transfer of value by Rory and Elizabeth. *1 mark*

1 mark

There is no interest in the trust subject to IHT for the other potential beneficiaries. *1 mark*

Total: 4 marks

(e) (i) The income from the fixed interest unit trust is made net of 20% tax. *1 mark*

A beneficiary who is a higher rate taxpayer is liable to pay an additional 20% income tax. *1 mark*

A beneficiary who is a basic rate taxpayer will have no further liability to income tax. *1 mark*

A beneficiary who is a starting rate taxpayer or non-taxpayer can recover all or some tax deducted at source. *1 mark*

(ii) The investments in the bond are subject to basic rate tax within the fund. *1 mark*

This tax can only be used to satisfy tax liability and cannot be repaid. *1 mark*

If Michael is alive at the date of the chargeable event, he will be assessable on the gain. *1 mark*

If Michael is a higher rate taxpayer, he will be liable to tax at 18%. *1 mark*

If Michael is not a higher rate taxpayer he will have no further liability. *1 mark*

If Michael is not alive at the date of the event, the trustees will be charged. *1 mark*

The trustees' rate of tax will be (40 – 22) = 18%. *1 mark*

Total: 11 marks

BPP
PROFESSIONAL EDUCATION

1 mark

(f) The nil rate band discretionary trust is set up to receive assets up to the remaining nil band at the date of Michael's death.

1 mark

At current values and rates and assuming Michael dies within 7 years of making the flexible trust, the value will be £(263,000 – 144,000) = £119,000.

1 mark

If Michael survives 7 years from making the trust, the amount would increase (at current values and rates) to £263,000.

1 mark

In both cases there would be no IHT to pay on the amount passing to the trust.

1 mark

The beneficiaries of the trust could include Julia, and Rory and Elizabeth and their children.

1 mark

The value of the trust would not be included in Julia's estate.

1 mark

However, the trustees could use the income (and/or capital) of the trust for Julia's benefit.

1 mark

If money was loaned to Julia, this would be a debt in her estate.

1 mark

Any outstanding amounts at Julia's death would reduce her estate and so save IHT.

1 mark

Any capital appointments after the first three months but before two years following Michael's death would not result in a exit charge.

1 mark

Any other capital appointments made within the first ten years of the trust's life would result in exit charges.

1 mark

However, the charge within the first ten years will be 0% because the initial value is within the nil band.

Total: 12 marks

1 mark

(g) If Rory and Elizabeth were alive at Michael's death, they would have to agree to make a variation.

1 mark

If either of them died and their children were not over the age of 18, the variation could not be made over that part of the estate.

1 mark

Rory and Elizabeth would have control over the terms of the variation, whereas Michael could specify the terms of the will trust.

1 mark

There is a strict time limit of two years for making the variation which could be missed.

1 mark

The parental income settlement rules would apply to a variation, but not to the will trust.

Total 6 marks

SECTION C

9   (a)   (i)   Jennifer's decision to work abroad will not affect her UK domicile.   *1 mark*

(ii)   The main tests of residency for Jennifer are: *1 mark*

- UK resident if spend at least 183 days in the UK.

- UK resident if visit UK regularly and these visits average 91 days or more a year for each of four or more consecutive tax years.   *2 marks*
1 mark

- UK resident if going abroad for occasional residence only (less than one tax year).   *Total: 4 marks*

(b)   (i)   The rental income will be taxable on Jennifer under Schedule A as UK source income.   *1 mark*

As a general principle, the letting agent or tenant must deduct basic rate tax from the property income.   *1 mark*
1 mark

Jennifer can apply to the Revenue to come within the self-assessment regime.   *1 mark*

The Revenue will then authorise the letting agent or tenant not to deduct tax.   *1 mark*

Jennifer can then receive the rental income gross.   *Total: 5 marks*

(ii)

	£	
Net rents	4,500	
Less: mortgage interest £35,000 × 8%	(2,800)	*1 mark*
Net income	1,700	*1 mark*

Note

A wear and tear allowance of 10% of gross rents may be available also, if the property is let furnished. Since the gross rent figure was not given in the question, it is not possible to calculate the amount of the deduction.   *1 mark*
Total: 4 marks

(c)   Exemption from capital gains tax is available for any period when the house is occupied as a principal private residence. In addition certain other periods are deemed to be periods of occupancy. These are: *1 mark*

- The last 36 months of ownership: and   *1 mark*

If the period of absence is followed by and preceded by a period of actual occupancy all of the following periods will be deemed to be periods of occupation: *1 mark*

- Any period(s) of absence for any reason totalling up to 3 years;   *1 mark*

- Any period of absence for any period that the home owner is required to live abroad by reason of her employment;   *1 mark*

- Any period of absence of up to 4 years when the homeowner is required to live elsewhere in the UK by reason of her work and is unable to occupy the property during that time.   *1 mark*
Total: 4 marks

(d)   (i)   The tax consequences of a distributor fund are:

- a UK resident investor is subject to income tax on distributions received   *1 mark*

- a UK resident investor is subject to CGT on the disposal of units   *1 mark*

- taper relief may be available to reduce the gain   *1 mark*
Total: 3 marks

BPP
PROFESSIONAL EDUCATION

(ii) The tax consequences of a non-distributor fund are:

1 mark

- the gain on a disposal of the units will be calculated in the same way as a capital gain.

1 mark

- no indexation allowance or taper relief is available.

1 mark

- the gain will be chargeable as income under Schedule D Case VI in the year of disposal of the units.

1 mark

Total: 4 marks

- if Jennifer is UK resident and a basic rate taxpayer in that year, she will suffer 22% tax on the gain.

(iii) The non-distributor fund will be more suitable for Jennifer.

1 mark

1 mark

She should encash the units whilst she is non-UK resident so that the income tax charge does not apply.

2 marks

Total: 4 marks

There may still be a charge to CGT on the disposal of the units, however, if she returns to the UK less than five years after the year of departure.

1 mark

(e) (i) The Spanish property will be subject to inheritance tax in Jennifer's estate.

1 mark

Total: 2 marks

This is because she is UK domiciled and her world-wide assets are therefore subject to inheritance tax.

(ii)

	£
1 mark	
1 mark ISA (note)	10,200
1 mark House in Spain	75,000
1 mark Cash at bank	158,800
1 mark House £(70,000 – 35,000)	35,000
1 mark Proceeds of endowment policy	35,000
1 mark Gross estate for IHT	314,000
1 mark IHT: £263,000 × 0%	
Total: 8 marks £51,000 × 40%	£20,400

Note The ISA value could also have been taken to include further contributions up to March 2004. However if Jennifer had become non resident or ordinarily resident in the UK she would no longer be eligible to invest in an ISA,

1 mark **10** (a) (i) For employees (not directors) earning less than £8,500 per tax year ('excluded employees'), benefits are generally taxed on their 'second hand value' (if any).

1 mark For employees earning £8,500 per tax year and directors, benefits are generally taxed on the cost to the employer of providing the benefit.

1 mark

Total: 3 marks There are some benefits which are taxable on all employees, eg. vouchers, accommodation, statutory mileage rates.

(ii) Cheap loans to employees earning £8,500 or over give rise to a benefit equal to any amounts written off and the excess of interest at the official rate over any interest actually charged.

1 mark

2 marks The interest benefit is calculated using either the average method (balances at the beginning and end of the tax year) or the strict method at the election of the taxpayer or the Revenue.

1 mark There is no benefit if the total on all loans to the employee does not exceed £5,000 at any time in the tax year.

Total: 4 marks

(b)   (i)   Taxable income for Christina

	Non savings income £	Savings income £	Dividend income £	Total income £	
Salary	24,210				*1 mark*
Car £14,100 × 25% (W)	3,525				*3 marks*
Fuel £14,400 × 25%	3,600				*2 marks*
BSI		1,600			*1 mark*
Divis from unit trust					*2 marks*
£2,475 × 100/90			2,750		
NS Bond £11,181 × 5.59%		625			*2 marks*
STI	31,335	2,225	2,750	36,310	*1 mark*
Less: PA	(4,745)			(4,745)	*1 mark*
Taxable income	26,590	2,225	2,750	31,565	*1 mark*

Working

195 – 145 = 50 ÷ 5 + basic % (15) = 25%

Tax

	£	
On non savings income		
£2,020 × 10%	202	*1 mark*
£(26,590 – 2,020) = £24,570 × 22%	5,405	*1 mark*
On savings income		
£2,225 × 20%	445	*1 mark*
On dividend income		
£(31,400 – 26,590 – 2,225) = 2,585 × 10%	259	*1 mark*
£(2,750 – 2,585) = 165 × 32.5%	54	*1 mark*
Total tax liability	6,365	*1 mark*
Less: deducted at source 2,750 × 10%	(275)	*1 mark*
Total tax payable (subject to PAYE already deducted)	6,090	*1 mark*

(ii)   National insurance contributions:

Total: 22 marks

£(24,210 – 4,745) = £19,465 subject to contributions   *1 mark*

Contributions at 11%   *1 mark*

£19,465 × 11% = £2,141   *1 mark*

Total: 3 marks

(c)

      WTC

1 mark	Basic	1,570
1 mark	Lone parent	1,545
1 mark	Childcare costs (restricted to £135 × 52 × 70%)	4,914
	Total	8,029

      CTC

1 mark	Family	545
1 mark	Child	1,625
1 mark	Disability	2,215
		4,385

	Annual income	8,250
	Less threshold	(5,060)
1 mark	Excess income	3,190
	Maximum credit (8,029+4,385)	12,414
	Less (37% × 3,190)	(1,180)
1 mark	Award	11,234

Total: 8 marks

11 (a)

		Non savings income £	Dividend income £	Total income £
1 mark	Sch DI	3,750		
1 mark	Rental income	6,800		
	Dividends £7,875 × 100/90		8,750	
	STI	10,550	8,750	19,300
2 marks	Less: AA (W)	(6,630)		(6,630)
1 mark	Taxable income	3,920	8,750	12,670

      Tax

		£
1 mark	*On non savings income*	
1 mark	£2,020 × 10%	202
	£(3,920 − 2,020) = £1,900 × 22%	418
	On dividend income	
1 mark	£8,750 × 10%	875
	Total tax liability	1,495

      Working

		£
2 marks	Age allowance	6,830
1 mark	Less: 1/2 × £(19,300 − 18,900)	(200)
	Reduced allowance	6,630

Total: 14 marks

(b) *C & F Investment Trust*

		Cost £	31.3.82MV £
2 marks	Proceeds	11,000	11,000
2 marks	Less: cost/31.3.82MV	(6,100)	(6,500)
2 marks	Unindexed gain	4,900	4,500
3 marks	Less: indexation allowance		
1 mark	1.047 × £6,500 = 6,805 restricted	(4,900)	(4,500)
	Indexed gain	nil	nil

Property

	£	
Proceeds	87,500	*1 mark*
Less: cost	(15,600)	*1 mark*
enhancement expenditure	(10,400)	*1 mark*
Unindexed gain	61,500	
Less: indexation allowance on cost		
0.922 × £15,600	(14,383)	*1 mark*
Indexation allowance on enhancement		
0.063 × £ 10,400	(655)	*1 mark*
Indexed gain	46,462	*1 mark*

Gain after taper relief (6.4.98 - 5.4.04 = 6 years plus additional year = 7 years)   *2 marks*

	£	
75% × £46,462	34,847	*1 mark*
Less: AE	(8,200)	*1 mark*
Taxable gain	26,647	*1 mark*

CGT

2 marks

2 marks

	£	
£(31,400 – 12,670) = £18,730 × 20%	3,746	
£(26,647 – 18,730) = £7,917 × 40%	3,167	*1 mark*
Tax payable	6,913	*Total: 26 marks*

Mock exam 2

ADVANCED FINANCIAL PLANNING CERTIFICATE
G10-TAXATION AND TRUSTS

SPECIAL NOTICES

- All questions in this paper are based on English law and practice applicable in the 2004/05 tax year, unless stated otherwise, and should be answered accordingly.

- Assume all individuals are domiciled, resident and ordinarily resident in the UK unless stated otherwise.

INSTRUCTIONS

- Three hours are allowed for this paper.

- **READ THE INSTRUCTIONS OVERLEAF CAREFULLY BEFORE ANSWERING ANY QUESTIONS.**

- If you wish to use a calculator in this examination, it must be a silent battery or solar powered calculator.

G10: Taxation and trusts

CANDIDATE INSTRUCTIONS

READ THE INSTRUCTRIONS BELOW BEFORE ANSWERING ANY QUESTIONS.

Three hours are allowed for this paper. You should answer all questions in Sections A and B, and two out of three questions in Section C.

The paper carries a total of 200 marks, as follows:

> Section A: 45 marks
> Section B: 75 marks
> Section C: 80 marks

You are advised to spend approximately 40 minutes on Section A, and 70 minutes each on Sections B and C. You are strongly advised to attempt ALL the required questions in order to gain maximum possible marks.

The number of marks allocated to each question part is given next to the question and you should spend your time in accordance with that allocation.

Tax tables are provided at the front of this kit.

Answer each question on a new page and leave several lines blank after each question part.

It is important to show all steps in a calculation, even if you have used a calculator.

Please ensure that you understand the Special Notices printed in the box on the previous page.

> *Subject to providing sufficient detail, you are advised to be as brief and concise as possible, using note format and short sentences on separate lines wherever possible.*

BPP
PROFESSIONAL EDUCATION

SECTION A

Answer all questions in this section, which carries 45 marks.

1   John is a married, self-employed builder who wants to provide for his family in the event of death by effecting a life assurance policy under trust.

   (a)   Briefly list the advantages of using a Married Women's Property Act Trust.   **(3)**

   (b)   Briefly list the advantages of using a flexible power of appointment trust instead.   **(3)**

2   Hugo aged 62, a UK resident carried forward a loss of £5,000 from the tax year 2003/04. During 2004/05 he made the following disposals.

12 May 2004	Gone South Investments plc	
	Proceeds	£4,000
	Cost	£6,000
	Indexation	£1,000
18 October 2004	East End Soaps plc	
	Proceeds	£24,500
	Cost	£12,000
	Indexation	£2,000

   Prepare a summary of Hugo's capital gains tax position for the year showing:

   (a)   the amount of capital gains on which tax is payable;   **(4)**

   (b)   and the amount of losses carried forward, if any, at 5 April 2005.   **(1)**

3   Explain fully how mutual wills operate.   **(6)**

4   Pearl, a 49 year old singer from Accrington, wants to give her 28 year old daughter Sonya her holding of zero dividend preference shares in North East Lancs Split Fund plc, bought in February 2000 and her holding of ordinary shares in the venture capital trust Rose Enterprises plc, for which she subscribed in November 2004.

   In relation to each proposed gift what, if any, are:

   (a)   the income tax consequences for Pearl?   **(2)**

   (b)   the capital gains tax consequences for Pearl?   **(5)**

5   Sydney aged 73, is a pensioner living in Edinburgh. On 3 March 2000 he invested £25,000 in an onshore five year guaranteed income bond issued by Terra Life plc, a UK insurance company. The bond provides income payments of £1,500 on 2 March each year up to and including 2 March 2005. On that date, Sydney's original investment of £25,000 is returned to him.

   Sydney's only other income is pension income of £14,000.

   (a)   **Showing all workings,** calculate the chargeable gain arising in 2004/05.   **(4)**

   (b)   Explain the potential disadvantages to Sydney of this type of investment.   **(2)**

6 (a) List the conditions for transfers to be allowed as normal expenditure and exempt for inheritance tax. **(4)**

(b) Explain how a back-to-back plan operates and how it relates to the normal expenditure rules. **(6)**

7 Colin Cromwell, aged 75 a retired meteorologist, established an accumulation and maintenance trust on 6 April 2004 for the benefit of his grandchildren. On 31 December 2004 the trust received building society interest of £16,000, this was the trust's only income in the tax year 2004/05. The trustees propose to make a payment of income to Miss Florence Fairfax (age 11) on 31 March 2005.

Calculate, showing **all workings**:

(a) the amount of income tax payable by the trust. **(4)**

(b) the maximum amount of income the trustees can pay to Florence without having to resort to capital in order to pay the trust's own income tax liability. **(1)**

SECTION B

This question is compulsory and carries 75 marks.

8   Until his death on 31 March 2005 Michael Thomas, aged 57, worked for the Global Insurance Company on a basic salary of £32,000 pa. He received private medical insurance with a P11D value of £1,500 pa. He was a member of the company's final salary pension scheme and paid a personal contribution of 5% pa. of his basic salary. In addition he paid a personal AVC contribution of £1,000 pa. which his employer matched. He was covered by death-in-service cover of four times basic salary and had nominated his only child Harry, aged 32, as his beneficiary.

Michael's first wife died in 1996. On 10 October 1997 using £261,000 life assurance paid out on her death, he set up a discretionary trust with his son Harry, Harry's wife Shirley and their three children as possible beneficiaries.

On 4 June 1998 Michael set up a single life qualifying unit-linked whole of life policy for a sum assured of £100,000 with an annual premium of £3,000 pa. The policy was written under a flexible power of appointment trust (excluding the settler as beneficiary) with his son Harry as the default beneficiary and his three children as the wider beneficial class. Michael and his sister Sue were appointed as the trustees. Sue was killed in a car accident in 2004 and no further trustee has been appointed.

On 1 November 2000 Michael set up a life interest trust with £150,000 cash he won on the National Lottery. His son Harry was the life tenant and Michael's grandchildren were the remaindermen.

In 2001 Michael married Barbara aged 50 and they agreed to keep their salaries and finances separate.

On 22 November 2003 an appointment was made under the flexible power of appointment trust, away from Harry to his three children in equal shares.

Under his will, Michael left his wife Barbara his personal chattels and a life interest in his house valued at £200,000 with his son Harry as the remainderman. His investments were left directly to Harry.

- Michael had an interest only mortgage of £30,000 on his house.
- He had no personal life assurance apart from the £100,000 whole of life plan.
- No other lifetime transfers were made by Michael.

The value of his investments at 31 March 2005 were:

	Value £	Gross Yield
Bank current account (No interest payable)	24,000	
Gilt 3 1/2 % funding 1999/05 (£10,000 Nominal)	9,600	
Wembley Building Society	10,000	7%
ISA*	8,400	6.75%
57th Issue National Savings Certificates	10,000	3.55%
PEPs*	55,000	6%
Anglo-French Investment Trust	54,000	9%
TOTAL	171,000	

*All income re-invested.

Relevant tax details

- The IHT nil rate band from 6.4.97 to 5.4.98 was £215,000
- The annual IHT exemption has been unchanged at £3,000 since 1985/86.

(a) Explain whether there was any IHT payable at the time of transfer(s) for **each** of the three trusts set up in Michael's lifetime. Calculate the tax payable where appropriate. **Show all your workings.** **(11)**

(b) Calculate the amount of income tax payable on Michael's income from all sources for tax year 2004/05. **Show all your workings.** **(25)**

(c) In respect of each of the three trusts which Michael had set up, explain if any further IHT is payable as a result of his death. Where appropriate, calculate the tax payable and state by whom it is payable.

   (i)   Discretionary trust set up on 10 October 1997. **(2)**

   (ii) Flexible power of appointment trust set up on 4 June 1998. **(2)**

   (iii) Life interest trust set up on 1 November 2000. **(12)**

(d) Calculate the IHT payable by Michael's executors in respect of his estate on death.

   (8)

(e) (i)   Explain the IHT consequences of the appointment of 22 November 2003 under the flexible power of appointment trust. **(8)**

   (ii) On Michael's death state who will be able to make a claim under the unit-linked whole of life plan and say what documentation they will require. **(7)**

Total marks available for Question 8: 75

SECTION C

Answer any two of the three questions in this section.

Each question carries 40 marks.

9   Jim Whitby's mother died three weeks ago. His father died three years ago and Jim now finds that his mother had not left a will. He has no brothers or sisters. Early indications are that there will be inheritance tax liabilities that could have been avoided. Jim wonders what might be done about this.

Jim is also concerned that he and his wife Judy have not made wills either. He tells you that he was married previously but divorced fifteen years ago. He has no children of his own by either his first or second marriage but he and Judy adopted Sarah, aged fourteen and Paul aged twelve, six years ago.

Jim tells you he is comfortably off and his home is valued at about £400,000. He owns this outright with Judy in equal proportion as 'tenants in common'. A friend advised him to buy his house this way to save tax but he doesn't know how it works.

Questions

(a)   Jim has read that a Deed of Variation may be of use to him in connection with his mother's intestacy. He is considering giving some of the money to his children, Sarah and Paul.

   (i)   Explain the taxation effects of such a Deed of Variation.   (7)

   (ii)   List the standard conditions that have to be met to ensure a Deed of Variation is legal and effective.   (9)

(b)   (i)   State the two possible legal consequences of the death of a tenant when a property is owned by 'tenants in common'.   (2)

   (ii)   State the actions Jim and Judy could take to utilise the tenancy in common of their property as a means of reducing their children's potential IHT liability.   (4)

   (iii)   State the main drawback of this solution.   (1)

(c)   (i)   State the legal position of adopted children in relation to their rights under the rules of intestacy.   (1)

   (ii)   State how divorce has affected Jim's former wife's rights under the rules of intestacy.   (1)

(d)   Explain how Jim's estate will be divided between Judy and the children if Jim dies before making a will.   (8)

(e)   Assume Jim and Judy make wills. List the processes the **executors** will need to follow on the **death** of either Jim or Judy.   (7)

Total marks available for Question 9: 40

10   Mr and Mrs Anderson are both in their late sixties and have two grandchildren twin girls aged 10. They have recently sold their large family home and have a sum of £120,000 which they wish to invest for their granddaughters. Even without this money their estate will be worth over £300,000 on their deaths, which is why they wish to make a gift of £120,000 now as they believe that doing so will save inheritance tax.

BPP
PROFESSIONAL EDUCATION

The Andersons also do not wish to hold the investments in their own names in the event that they should die before the grandchildren attain the age of 18. They would ideally like the girls to have access to both the income and the capital at the age of 18 to assist with university education or the purchase of houses. They hope that the girls will have sufficient capability to manage their own money at that stage.

(a) Outline briefly the role of the trustees in:

    (i)   an Accumulation and Maintenance Trust. **(3)**

    (ii)   a Bare Trust. **(2)**

(b) Mr and Mrs Anderson are considering setting up a trust for their granddaughters. Explain the tax treatment of

    (i)   an Accumulation and Maintenance Trust. **(10)**

    (ii)   a Bare Trust. **(7)**

(c) Explain the tax treatment of

    (i)   an Accumulation and Maintenance Trust investing in a single premium life assurance distribution bond, managed by a UK based life assurance company. **(9)**

    (ii)   a Bare Trust investing in an onshore OEIC umbrella fund. **(9)**

Total marks available for Question 10: 40

11   Harold Thomas is aged 65, who is a widower. He acquired a holding of shares in ABC plc (a quoted company) on his uncle's death eight years ago. Harold also has substantial cash deposits.

Harold wishes to provide for his children, Janet and George (who are in their mid-thirties) and their children. Harold has made no previous lifetime gifts. He has been advised by his solicitor to set up a discretionary trust. Harold will transfer his shares (now worth £165,000) to the trust, plus cash of £100,000 in March 2005. Harold wants to pay as little tax as possible on the creation of the trust.

The cash will be invested by the trustees in a high interest building society account.

Part of the income of the trust may be paid out to George, whose business is struggling.

Harold envisages that a capital lump sum will be required by Janet in a couple of years' time. The trustees would probably appoint part of the holding of ABC plc shares to Janet at that time.

Questions

(a) Describe the inheritance tax and capital gains tax consequences of the creation of the discretionary trust. **(17)**

(b) Explain the interest and dividends generated by the investments in the trust will be taxed in the hands of the trustees. **(6)**

(c) Describe how the income tax treatment of the income payments to George for both the trustees and George. **(10)**

(d) Explain the inheritance tax and capital gains tax implications of the appointment of capital to Janet. **(7)**

Total marks available for Question 11: 40

Advanced Financial Planning Certificate

G10

Answers
to
Mock Exam 2

Overview of Mock Examination 2

Section A

There were two law questions and five tax questions in this section. Generally the topics covered should have been familiar, although question 3 on Mutual Wills may have caught you out. It was important to give a reasonable amount of detail to obtain good marks on the written questions and answer the question as set, rather than state general points.

Question 5 dealt with the ever popular single premium bond. This area of the syllabus is heavily examined and you should study the solution carefully.

Section B

This was the usual 'death' question bringing in various aspects of IHT and income tax.

There were no particular difficulties in the question. However, if you have had problems with lifetime IHT transfers, you should rework the solution of parts (a) and (c).

It should have been possible to get full (or nearly full!) marks on the income tax part if the correct layout was used - make sure you know this very well.

The law element in part (e)(ii) would have been difficult to score full marks on.

Section C

A choice of two out of three questions to be answered.

Question 9 was a written question on variations and wills. Not a favourite area for students, but it should be possible to pick up reasonable marks on the conditions required for variations. Some common sense marks were also available on the position of an adopted child and a former spouse.

Question 10 was on trusts. Some quite basic points on IHT and CGT would have given reasonable marks. Again, study the solution for any additional points. The taxation of investments is almost always examined and is often an area of weakness. One way to revise this area would be to make a list of different investments and outline the main income tax and capital gains consequences of each.

Question 11 was about CGT and IHT on transfers of assets plus the set up of a discretionary trust.

ANSWERS TO MOCK EXAM 2

SECTION A

1   (a)   The advantages of using a Married Women's Property Act Trust are:

        (i)   it is simple to set up as a standard trust form issued by the life office can be used. *1 mark*

        (ii)   it provides good protection from creditors of the assured. *1 mark*

        (iii)   it has clearly defined categories of beneficiaries (spouse and children of the assured). *1 mark*

        Total: 3 marks

   (b)   The advantages of using a non-statutory flexible power of appointment trust are:

        (i)   the policy written in trust does not have to be a single policy on the life of the assured (eg could be joint life). *1 mark*

        (ii)   a wider range of beneficiaries is possible than with a Married Women's Property Act trust. *1 mark*

        (iii)   the trust can be written flexibly eg. to allow a change of beneficiaries, varying of entitlements. *1 mark*

        Total: 3 marks

2   (a)

	£	
Gone South shares		
Proceeds	4,000	
Less: cost	(6,000)	*1 mark*
Loss	(2,000)	
East End shares		
Proceeds	24,500	
Less: cost	(12,000)	
Unindexed gain	12,500	
Less: indexation allowance	(2,000)	
Indexed gain	10,500	*1 mark*

	£	
Gain of year	10,500	
Less: current year loss	(2,000)	
Net gains of year	8,500	
Less: loss b/f £(8,500 – 8,200)	(300)	*1 mark*
Net gain	8,200	
[Technically taper relief would apply to this net gain at this stage]		
Less: annual exemption	(8,200)	*1 mark*
Taxable gain	nil	*Total: 4 marks*

   (b)   Loss c/f £(5,000 – 300) £4,700 *1 mark*

3   Under the doctrine of mutual wills, two persons (often husband and wife) make an agreement that their property is to devolve in a certain way. *2 marks*

For example, the agreement may specify that on the first of them to die, the deceased's property passes to the survivor, and after his or her death, the property of both of them passes to nominated beneficiaries, such as their children. *2 marks*

The law will allow the ultimate beneficiaries to enforce the agreement. *1 mark*

In essence a constructive trust arises of which the survivor is trustee. *1 mark*

Total: 6 marks

4 (a) There are no income tax implications on the gift of the zero dividend preference shares.

1 mark

The income tax relief given on the venture capital trust shares will be withdrawn.

1 mark
Total: 2 marks

(b) The zero dividend preference shares will be disposed of at market value for capital gains tax purposes.

1 mark

The disposal may result in a gain or a loss.

1 mark

A gain may be reduced by losses on other disposals and the annual exemption.

1 mark

The disposal of the shares in the venture capital trust will not result in a chargeable gain nor allowable loss.

2 marks
Total: 5 marks

5 (a) Profit taxable 2004/05

	£	£
Proceeds		25,000
Income payments 1,500 × 5 years	7,500	
Less: assessed in earlier years		
£1,500 – (5% × £25,000) = 250 × 4	(1,000)	6,500
		31,500
Less: cost		(25,000)
Gain now chargeable		6,500

1 mark
1 mark
1 mark
1 mark
Total: 4 marks

(b) The deferred allowances come back into charge in the year of the repayment of the bond instead of being spread out over the bond's life.

1 mark

The age allowance limit is therefore exceeded and Sydney's age allowance is therefore reduced (no top slicing available as full bond profit must be included).

1 mark
Total: 2 marks

6 (a) A transfer of value is exempt from inheritance tax as normal expenditure out of income if:

(i) it is made as part of the normal expenditure of the transferor (ie. regular/habitual).

2 marks

(ii) taking one year with another, it was made out of income.

1 mark

(iii) it leaves the transferor with sufficient income to maintain his usual standard of living.

1 mark
Total: 4 marks

(b) A back to back plan works as follows:

(i) a lump sum is paid, most of which is used to purchase an immediate annuity, with the balance used for the first premium.

1 mark

(ii) a whole of life policy is taken out either with another life office or properly underwritten (to avoid associated operations problems for IHT).

1 mark

(iii) the whole of life policy is written in trust.

1 mark

(iv) the net income from the annuity is used to pay the premium on the whole of life policy.

1 mark

(v) the payment of the premium is a transfer of value for IHT purposes but the amount equivalent to interest content of the annuity can be treated as normal expenditure out of income.

1 mark

(vi) the annuity ceases on death and the whole of life policy pays out tax-free to the beneficiaries.

1 mark
Total: 6 marks

7   (a)

BSI £16,000 × 100/80	<u>£20,000</u>	*1 mark*
	£	
Tax @40% on £20,000	8,000	*1 mark*
Less: tax deducted at source	(4,000)	*1 mark*
Tax payable under self assessment by trustees	<u>4,000</u>	*1 mark*

Total: 4 marks

(b) Amount available for distribution to Florence:

Net income £(16,000 – 4,000)	<u>12,000</u>	*1 mark*

SECTION B

8 (a) Inheritance tax on lifetime transfers

		£

1 mark   10.10.97 Transfer to discretionary trust
           (chargeable lifetime transfer)   261,000

1 mark   Less: AE 1997/98   (3,000)

1 mark   AE 1996/97 b/f   (3,000)

                                     255,000

1 mark   IHT: £215,000 × 0%

1 mark   £40,000 × 1/4 (assumes transferor paid tax)   10,000

1 mark   Gross transfer &(255,000 + 10,000)   265,000

2 marks   4.6.98   Payment of premiums of £3,000 pa will be exempt because of the annual exemption, or possibly, the normal expenditure out of income exemption.

1 mark   1.11.00   Transfer to life interest trust for son is a potentially exempt transfer.

1 mark   No lifetime tax due.

1 mark   Assume that AEs used by premium payments.

Total: 11 marks

(b)

	Non savings income £	Savings income £	Dividend Income £	Total income
1 mark Salary	32,000			
1 mark Medical insurance	1,500			
	33,500			
2 marks Less: pension 5%	(1,600)			
1 mark AVC	(1,000)			
1 mark No benefit for employer's contribution				
2 marks Gilt interest £10,000 × 3.5%		350		
2 marks BSI £10,000 × 7%		700		
Anglo French investment trust				
2 marks £54,000 × 9%			4,860	
1 mark STI	30,900	1,050	4,860	36,810
2 marks Less: PA	(4,745)			(4,745)
1 mark Taxable income	26,155	1,050	4,860	32,065

	£
Tax	
On non savings income	
1 mark £2,020 × 10%	202
2 marks £(26,155 – 2,020) = £24,135 × 22%	5,310
On savings income	
1 mark £1,050 × 20%	210
On dividend income	
2 marks £(31,400 – 26,155 – 1,050) = 4,195 × 10%	420
2 marks £(4,860 – 4,195) = 665 × 32.5%	216
1 mark Total tax liability	6,358

Total: 25 marks

1 mark   (c) (i)   There is no further tax liability on the transfer to the discretionary trust on 10 October 1997.

1 mark   This is because Michael has survived seven years from the transfer.

Total: 2 marks

1 mark   (ii)   There is no death tax on the policy in the flexible power of appointment trust.

This is because the policy is written in trust and does not form part of the death estate.

1 mark

Total: 2 marks

(iii) PET made on 1 November 2000 becomes chargeable

2 marks

Gift/gross transfer   £150,000

2 marks

Tax

	£	
Transfer of £265,000 in October 1997 has used up NRB		*2 marks*
£150,000 × 40%	60,000	*2 marks*
Death tax		*1 mark*
Less: taper relief (4 to 5 years) £60,000 × 40%	(24,000)	*2 marks*
Death tax payable by the trustees	36,000	*1 mark*
		Total: 12 marks

(d) Death estate

	£	£	
House	200,000		*1 mark*
Less: mortgage	(30,000)		*1 mark*
Net value of house	170,000		
Less: spouse exemption	(170,000)	nil	*1 mark*
Value of investments		171,000	*1 mark*
Chargeable estate		171,000	*1 mark*

Tax

	£	
£(263,000 – 150,000) = £113,000 × 0%	nil	*1 mark*
£(171,000 – 113,000) = 58,000 × 40%	23,200	*1 mark*
Tax on death estate	23,200	*1 mark*
		Total: 8 marks

(e) (i) As default beneficiary, Harry had an interest in possession in the trust when it was set up.

1 mark

The removal of the interest in possession is deemed to be a transfer of value by Harry.

1 mark

The amount of the transfer is the greater of the total premiums paid and the open market value of the policy.

1 mark

As the new beneficiaries are Harry's children, the transfer of value is likely to be a potentially exempt transfer (depending on the nature of the trust for the children eg if accumulation and maintenance trust).

2 marks

If the transfer is a potentially exempt transfer and Harry survives seven years, there will be no inheritance tax implications.

1 mark

If Harry dies within seven years, his exemptions and previous transfers at the date of the transfer will be used to calculate the extent to which the transfer is taxable.

2 marks

Total: 8 marks

(ii) As a general principle, the trustees of the trust would make a claim under the policy on Michael's death.

1 mark

However, in this case both the original trustees have died.

1 mark

The executors of a sole surviving trustee (ie. Michael) become trustees.

1 mark

The documents required will therefore be:

- death certificate of Sue

1 mark

- death certificate of Michael

1 mark

- grant of probate of Michael, showing executors

1 mark

1 mark
1 mark
Total: 8 marks
(max 7)

- policy
- trust deed

SECTION C

1 mark

9 (a) (i) If a deed of variation and the appropriate statement are made by Jim, the disposition of property made in the variation is treated as having been made by Jim's mother and taxed accordingly.

1 mark

1 mark   There is no transfer of value by Jim.

1 mark

If a Deed of Variation is made and the appropriate statement made by Jim, the property subject to the variation is treated as passing at probate value to Sarah and Paul for CGT purposes.

1 mark

There is no disposal by Jim.

1 mark

There are no provisions dealing with income tax so any income arising up to the date of variation will be taxed on Jim.

1 mark
Total: 7 marks

Jim will be treated as the settlor of the property on his minor children.

Therefore any income in excess of £100 pa for each child will be taxed on Jim.

2 marks   (ii) The beneficiary making the variation must be over the age of eighteen and sane.

1 mark   The variation must be made in writing.

1 mark   It must be made within two years of the death of the deceased.

1 mark   There must not be consideration for making the variation.

4 marks

The variation must include a statement that the provision is to apply, made by the beneficiary and the personal representatives of the deceased (if more IHT is due as a result of the variation).

Total: 9 marks

(b) (i) On the death of a tenant in common, his share passes with his estate.

1 mark

1 mark   The share therefore passes under the Will or intestacy of the deceased.

Total: 2 marks   (ii) Jim and Judy could make wills.

Under the wills they could leave their shares in the property to their children.

1 mark

1 mark   This would use up their nil rate bands for inheritance tax.

1 mark   Alternatively, a nil rate band discretionary trust could be used.

1 mark   (iii) This solution might reduce the security of the surviving spouse in the house.

Total: 4 marks
1 mark

(c) (i) Adopted children are treated as children of the adoptive parents, not their natural parents.

1 mark   (ii) An ex-spouse has no rights under the rules of intestacy.

1 mark   (d) If Jim dies without making a will (intestate), the following rules apply.

3 marks

Judy will be entitled to personal chattels, cash or assets worth £125,000 and a life interest in half of residue.

2 marks

The children will be entitled to the other half of residue and the reversionary interest in the half of residue in which Judy has a life interest.

2 marks   The entitlements of the children will be held in trust until they attain the age of 18.
Total: 8 marks

(e) Complete an inheritance tax account (including details of lifetime transfers made) and pay any IHT due.

2 marks

Obtain a Grant of Probate.

1 mark

Collect in the assets of the estate.

1 mark

Settle the liabilities of the estate (funeral expenses, tax, lifetime liabilities, expenses of administration).

2 marks

Pay out the remainder of the estate to the beneficiaries in accordance with the terms of the will.

1 mark
Total: 7 marks

10 (a) (i) The trustees in an Accumulation and Maintenance (A&M) Trust:

- collect income and decide whether or not to use the income for the maintenance, education or benefit of the beneficiaries under the 'specified age' (see below).

1 mark

- accumulate (make into capital) any income not so used.

1 mark

- pay out income to beneficiaries who have attained the specified age (which must not exceed the age of 25).

1 mark

- apply capital, at their discretion, for the advancement of beneficiaries.

1 mark
Total: 4 marks
(max 3)

(ii) The trustees of a Bare Trust:

- hold the income and capital of the trust for the beneficiaries.

1 mark

- until those beneficiaries attain the age of 18, when they can discharge the trustees from their duties.

1 mark

- effectively the trustees act as nominees for the beneficiaries.

1 mark
Total: 3 marks
(max 2)

(b) (i) The creation of an A&M trust is a potentially exempt transfer for IHT purposes.

1 mark

Non-dividend income in the trust will be taxed at the rate of 40%, less any tax deducted at source.

1 mark

Dividend income in the trust will be taxed at 32.5%, less the tax credit of 10%, giving a net payment of 22.5%.

1 mark

The trustees will have a pool of tax to give tax credits on income payments to beneficiaries.

1 mark

The tax pool will consist of tax at 40% on non-dividend income and 32.5% on dividend income.

1 mark

All income payments to beneficiaries must be given a 40% tax credit.

1 mark

The beneficiaries can then reclaim the tax, using their own personal allowances and rates of tax to calculate their liability.

1 mark

The trustees can claim taper relief on gains made by them, in a similar way to individuals.

1 mark

The trustees have a capital gains tax annual exemption of $1/2$ of the individual exemption ($1/2 \times £8,200 = £4,100$).

1 mark

The trustees pay capital gains tax at 40% on any remaining gains.

1 mark

There is no further charge to capital gains tax on proceeds of sale appointed to beneficiaries.

Total: 11 marks
(max 10)

1 mark	(ii)	The creation of a Bare Trust is a potentially exempt transfer.
1 mark		The income of the trust is treated as that of the beneficiaries as their own income.
1 mark		The beneficiaries own personal allowances and rates of tax are therefore used to calculate any further income tax due.
1 mark		There are no income tax implications if income is used for the benefit of the beneficiaries.
1 mark		Taper relief is available on capital gains as the gains are treated as those of the beneficiaries.
1 mark		The beneficiaries annual exemptions can be used against trust gains.
1 mark *Total: 7 marks*		The rate of capital gains tax on remaining gains depends on the income of the beneficiaries ie. 10%, 20% or 40%.

(c) (i) *1 mark* — As this is not an offshore bond, the underlying fund is taxed on its income and gains at 20%/22% depending on the underlying investments.

1 mark — Further income tax may be suffered if a chargeable event occurs (encashment of policy due to surrender, sale or death of life assured).

3 marks — If the settlor is alive immediately before the time of the chargeable event, the gain is deemed to form part of the settlor's total income for the year in which the event occurred and is taxed accordingly.

2 marks — If the settlor is dead or non-resident immediately before the time of the chargeable event and the policy is held by UK resident trustees in an accumulation and maintenance trust, the gain is deemed to form part of the income of the trustees for that year and is taxed at the rate applicable to trusts in that year.

1 mark — In both cases, a notional basic rate tax credit is given.

1 mark *Total: 9 marks* — The tax paid by the trustees does not enter the tax pool and therefore is not available for tax credits for the beneficiaries.

(ii) *1 mark* — The OEIC is not taxed on gains or UK source dividend income and suffers tax at 20% on other income.

1 mark — All the income of the OEIC is taxed as that of the members whether paid out to them or not.

1 mark — The OEIC can decide whether such income is treated as a dividend or as interest.

1 mark — For this purpose, as this is a bare trust, the grandchildren will be treated as the members and so can use their personal allowances and rates of tax in calculating their tax liability.

1 mark — A capital gain or loss will arise on a disposal of the shares in the OEIC.

1 mark — Capital gains will be taxed on the grandchildren.

1 mark *Total: 9 marks* — There will be no further tax payable on distributions of income or capital to the beneficiaries.

11 (a) The transfer of assets to the discretionary trust is a chargeable lifetime transfer. *1 mark*

The value of the gift is £265,000. *1 mark*

Harold will be entitled to two annual exemptions of £3,000 each. *1 mark*

The chargeable total is £259,000. *1 mark*

This is within the nil rate band of £263,000. *1 mark*

There will be no lifetime inheritance tax to pay. *1 mark*

There will also be no additional tax to pay if Harold dies within seven years. *1 mark*

However, £259,000 of the Harold's nil band will be used up until he survives this seven year period. *1 mark*

The disposal of the ABC plc shares is a chargeable disposal for CGT. *1 mark*

The gain will be the difference between the market value of the shares at settlement and the value of the shares at the uncle's death. *1 mark*

Indexation allowance will be deducted for the period between the uncle's death and April 1998. *1 mark*

Harold can make a gift relief election to pass the gain to the trustees. *1 mark*

This is because the transfer is a chargeable lifetime transfer for IHT. *1 mark*

The claim must be made by 31 January 2011. *1 mark*

If Harold makes a gift relief election, no taper relief will be available to reduce the heldover gain. *1 mark*

The trustees will start a new ownership period for taper relief. *1 mark*

Cash is not a chargeable asset for CGT so there are no CGT implications. *1 mark*

(b) Interest will be grossed up at 20% to take account of the tax deducted at source. *1 mark*

The interest will be subject to 40% tax in the hands of the trustees. *1 mark*

The trustees can set the 20% tax deducted at source against their liability. *1 mark*

Dividend income will be grossed up at 10%. *1 mark*

The dividend income will be subject to 32.5% tax in the hands of the trustees. *1 mark*

The trustees can set the 10% tax credit against this liability. *1 mark*

(c) The income payment to George must be grossed up by 40%. *1 mark*

The trustees are liable to 40% tax on the payment. *1 mark*

The trustees can set the 40% tax paid by them on the interest against this liability. *1 mark*

They can also set 22.5% additional tax paid by them on the dividends against this liability. *1 mark*

They cannot set the 10% tax credit on the dividends against this liability. *1 mark*

The gross income payment will be taxable on George as non-savings income. *1 mark*

George will be liable to tax on the payment at 10%, 22% or 40%. *1 mark*

This depends on the rest of his income and to the extent that it exceeds his personal allowance. *1 mark*

George can set the 40% tax credit against his tax liability *1 mark*

He can reclaim any excess tax paid. *1 mark*

(d) The appointment of capital to Janet will trigger an exit charge for IHT.

The initial value of the trust is £259,000.

Since this is within the nil band, there will be no liability to IHT on the exit as it is before the first ten year charge.

The appointment of the ABC plc shares will be a disposal by the trustees at market value for CGT.

The gain arising can be passed to Janet by a gift relief election.

The election must be effected by the trustees and Janet making a joint election.

This is because the disposal is an exit charge for IHT, even though no IHT is actually payable.

The taper clock will again be restarted by the transfer to Janet.